SAVE A FORTUNE ON YOUR ESTATE TAXES

Other Books By Barry Kaye
How to Save a Fortune
on Your Life Insurance

SAVE A FORTUNE ON YOUR ESTATE TAXES

Wealth Creation and Preservation

Barry Kaye

FORMAN PUBLISHING, INC.
Santa Monica

Library of Congress Cataloging-in-Publication Data

Kaye, Barry, 1928–
    Save a fortune on your estate taxes.

    Includes index.
    1. Inheritance and transfer tax — Law and legislation — United States.   2. Tax planning — United States.   3. Estate planning — United States.   4. Insurance, Life — United States.   I. Title.
KF6588.K39   1990   343.7305′3   90-3349
ISBN 0-936614-10-2 (alk. paper)   347.30353

Printed in the United States of America

10   9   8   7   6   5   4   3   2   1

*This book is dedicated
to my loving wife, Carole,
who shares my vision.
Her support and
understanding make it
all possible.*

Uncle Sam Comes First

Up to 55% of Your Life's Worth is Going to Go to One Grateful Relative – Your Uncle Sam

$5 MILLION

So you've made $5 million in your lifetime. After you paid income taxes your net worth is $3.3 million. After your children pay estate taxes upon your death, it will be worth $2,037,000. After your grandchildren pay estate taxes upon the death of your children, it will be worth $1,468,650. Your estate will be worth 29% of its original value after only two generations of taxation. You will have lost 71%, for a total loss of $3,531,350.

$20 MILLION

So you've made $20 million in your lifetime. After you paid income taxes your net worth is $13.2 million. After your children pay estate taxes upon your death, it will be worth $6,332,000. After your grandchildren pay estate taxes upon the death of your children, it will be worth $3,401,400. Your estate will be worth 17% of its original value after only two generations of taxation. You will have lost 83%, for a total loss of $16,598,600.

$50 MILLION

So you've made $50 million in your lifetime. After you paid income taxes your net worth is $33 million. After your children pay estate taxes upon your death, it will be worth $14,850,000. After your grandchildren pay estate taxes upon the death of your children, it will be worth $6,992,000. Your estate will be worth 14% of its original value after only two generations of taxation. You will have lost 86%, for a total loss of $43,008,000.

The Cost of Estate Taxation Means Estate Decimation

$100 MILLION

So you've made $100 million in your lifetime. After you paid income taxes your net worth is $66 million. After your children pay estate taxes upon your death, it will be worth $29.7 million. After your grandchildren pay estate taxes upon the death of your children, it will be worth $13,365,000. Your estate will be worth 13% of its original value after only two generations of taxation. You will have lost 87%, for a total loss of $86,665,000.

$500 MILLION

So you've made $500 million in your lifetime. After you paid income taxes your net worth is $330 million. After your children pay estate taxes upon your death, it will be worth $148.5 million. After your grandchildren pay estate taxes upon the death of your children, it will be worth $66,825,000. Your estate will be worth 13% of its original value after only two generations of taxation. You will have lost 87%, for a total loss of $433,175,000.

$1 BILLION

So you've made $1 billion in your lifetime. After you paid income taxes your net worth is $660 million. After your children pay estate taxes upon your death, it will be worth $297 million. After your grandchildren pay estate taxes upon the death of your children, it will be worth $133,633,000. Your estate will be worth 13% of its original value after only two generations of taxation. You will have lost 87%, for a total loss of $866,347,000.

There is a way to replace this loss. And in this book, I will show you what it is.

Contents

A Note from the Publisher

Estate taxation is a very complex subject, and generalizations are not applicable to everyone. It is important that your own specific situation be analyzed by an attorney, accountant, tax specialist, and qualified life insurance specialist. If legal advice or other expert opinion is required, the services of a competent professional should be sought.

In this book the author describes situations in which all of the facts were available to him. Without knowledge of your specific requirements, the author and the publisher disclaim any liability for loss incurred by the use of any direct or indirect application of the material contained herein.

Throughout this book, the approach detailed will frequently be referred to as an "investment." While not commonly recognized as an investment per se, this approach nevertheless does produce a substantial return much in excess of whatever you put into it. And because of the tax advantages inherent in the approach, it further produces results comparable to and way beyond those of any other prudent, conservative investment of this type.

The phrase "based on current assumptions" is used throughout the book to qualify the specific results illustrated by the given examples. Results can only be guaranteed as long as the mortality and interest assumptions used to determine them remain the

11

same. Any changes in the basic assumptions will alter the specific results, or returns. In most cases, the results would still be superior to those realized through any other approach.

Guarantees of results are also limited by the assumed solvency of the company or consortium of companies participating in the program.

In all examples given in this book, the author has taken the liberty of eliminating the cost of money from all proposals and projections. This eliminates lengthy and unnecessary discussion about the "internal rate of return." In all cases cited as examples, he has diversified his client's portfolio and, in most cases, utilized less than 10% of the client's assets in doing so. More important, he has never proposed any course of financial action that would adversely affect his client's lifestyle; therefore the internal rate of return is irrelevant in the context of the benefits that these programs provide.

Acknowledgments

There are several individuals without whose professional expertise, invaluable assistance and personal caring this book would not have been possible.

To my contributing editor, Rhonda Morstein, goes my heartfelt thanks and my highest esteem. Her quick grasp of complex and often difficult concepts and her ability to then communicate those concepts clearly and concisely makes this book both accurate and readable. Her involvement helped make this project a pleasure instead of a chore.

Further thanks to Deborah Daly. Her handling of the design for the book jacket and text was a perfect blend of professionalism and creativity. She captured our intent in all her efforts and succeeded brilliantly against the constraints of scheduling.

Special acknowledgment also to Lynette Padwa for her careful, precise editing. Lynette's comprehension of technical intricacies was both impressive and invaluable.

My thanks also go out to Michael Martin for his expertise in creating all the charts which appear in this book. They are a tremendous help in making this often complicated material easier to understand.

To my publisher, Len Foreman, goes my personal thanks and appreciation. Len is a friend of long-standing, a knowledgeable advisor, consummate professional and skilled publisher.

I would also like to acknowledge the on-going contributions of The Weston Group. They have aided my efforts in various endeavors over the years with great responsiveness and creativity.

And, of course, my most sincere thanks to my many associates here and at the Barry Kaye affiliated network of Wealth Creation Center offices who provide continuous help and inspiration through the time, energy, spirit and vision they contribute so unstintingly.

1

Why I Wrote This Book

In the Academy Award-winning movie *Moonstruck*, there is a scene in which Olympia Dukakis is sitting in her living room waiting for her husband to come home. Over the last few days she has repeatedly quizzed everyone she has come in contact with as to why a man cheats on his wife. She finally gets the answer from her daughter's fiancé. Men cheat, he says, because they are afraid of dying. That night when her husband, Cosmo, comes home, she looks him straight in the eye and says, "Cosmo, I just want you to know, no matter what you do, you're gonna die just like everybody else."

The point is that few things in life are guaranteed. One of them is death. No matter what happens, we are all going to die someday.

The second guarantee is estate taxes. No one, including your attorney, financial planner, accountant, or stockbroker, can change that. You are going to pay estate taxes. It's unavoidable unless you plan to give all your money to charity. That is a very noble undertaking, but people who have spent a lifetime building their assets will almost assuredly want their children, grandchildren, other family members, and future progeny to enjoy the opportunities afforded by a secure financial position.

As caretaker of your family's future, you want to establish a means by which they can provide for future generations in addition to endowing those charitable institutions you favor. While it is inevitable that your family must someday suffer the loss of your presence, you want to make certain that estate taxes do not deprive them of all you have dedicated your life to amassing.

My job in this book is to show you how to do that — to demonstrate how you can insure the continuation of your legacy.

Given that death and estate taxes are guaranteed, I can show you how to make the inevitable estate tax costs only 10 or 50 cents on the dollar of what they will be otherwise... effectively reducing your estate tax costs by as much as 80% to 90%, thereby reserving more money to create and preserve financial security for your loved ones.

Believe it or not, it's true, it's real, it works, and best of all, it's completely legal and beneficial to all involved parties. For a minimum investment — often no more than 10% of what your estate tax would otherwise be — your estate can realize a guaranteed return that is estate tax free and can be used to reduce your estate taxes to that minimal 10% investment cost.

If I told you that there was a building under construction and you could invest in it for $500,000, and that when the building was finished *your $500,000 investment would be guaranteed to be worth $5 million*, wouldn't you want to make that investment? If I further told you that the $5 million could come to your estate tax free and could be used to offset your estate tax costs so that the next generation effectively suffered no depletion of worth, wouldn't you want to know where this building is and how to invest in it? Well, metaphorically speaking, such a building does exist and I'm going to show you where it is and how you can share in this fantastic investment opportunity.

However, before we continue, we must consider for whom this investment is best suited. While we would all like to take advantage of great opportunities such as this one, not everyone is in a position to do so.

Certainly everyone wants to pass along as much as they can

to future generations. But life is for the living, and if the initial investment required means that you must suffer a decline in lifestyle in order to provide for future heirs, I would not recommend that the investment be made.

Let's say a man has three children whom he loves very much. In addition, he has four grandchildren who are a true joy to him. But as much as this man loves his children and grandchildren, and as much as he wants to provide for their welfare, he loves his wife more, and her welfare is of paramount importance. If investing $500,000 in the building mentioned earlier means that he and his wife's lifestyle must suffer, he should not make that investment even though to do so would benefit his children by $5 million. Even if it's $250,000 or $100,000 or less, if investing that money would result in a significant decline in current lifestyle, I would not recommend doing so.

If, however, your estate is such that the income it generates would be more than sufficient to assure your continued lifestyle even minus the initial investment amount, then what better use could you put that additional money to than as an investment with a guaranteed return that will insure the financial security of future generations by effectively reducing the tax they must pay on your estate by 80% to 90%?

Naturally, if you are living on the income from $10 million and need the income from $15 million to satisfy your lifestyle, this program is not for you. Or, looking at it another way, if you are making $500,000 a year on your investments and living on $700,000, you cannot afford to participate.

However, if you are earning $300,000 a year from your investments and living on only $160,000, then you have excess money available to you. Or, if you have $10 million and are only living on the income from $5 million, leaving you another $5 million to invest, the program described in this book could be better than any new investment you might make. This is true for many people. And still many of those people rush around from bank to bank searching for an extra ¼% of interest on the difference. But in the long run, that increased ¼% of interest will mean only a very slight true increase in total value —an increase that will, itself, be halved by estate taxation.

Using the wealth creation techniques detailed in this book, that same excess money could be used to earn a return of as much as 10 or even 20 times the original investment — and the money would come to the estate tax free.

The means to do this will be explained in detail in this book. You will learn exactly how to protect your estate from the devastation of estate tax costs. My plan is not complicated, but it is new and dramatic. Many people who have not heard of this method or don't fully comprehend it will be skeptical. But it does work, it is legal, and it is completely guaranteed, based on current assumptions.

If you are currently worth $1 million, $3 million, $10 million, $50 million, $100 million, $300 million, $500 million, or even $1 billion, your estate can benefit from this plan in ways that no other means will provide. *There exists no other method that legally permits and guarantees the results you will certainly realize from this investment.*

Even if you are a young married couple, 40 years of age, with a $2 million estate, you have an estate tax liability of approximately $600,000. But that just represents today's liability. What happens 30 years from now? Let us assume a 5% annual growth of your estate for the next 30 years — you will find your estate will eventually be worth over $8.5 million with a resulting federal estate tax liability of approximately $4 million.

Whether this appreciation is applied to current assets of only $1 million or we use the aforementioned estate sizes of $3 million to $1 billion and apply future appreciation and inflation, the far-reaching ramifications of your family's future estate tax liability should become readily apparent. You actually are worth only 45% of what you think, and the situation will compound over the balance of your lifetime.

In the following pages I will show you exactly what your tax exposure is and demonstrate to you the hazards of unprotected wealth. I will then show you how to protect your estate to create and preserve wealth for future generations. I will use charts and tables to show you how you and your family can benefit and what costs and returns your current financial situation will yield. I will examine the role of your other advisors and consultants and will offer expert testimony to verify my claims.

What better peace of mind could you ask for than a method that guarantees the future protection of your estate and your family? In this book, you will discover the means to truly preserve for your loved ones the wealth it took you a lifetime to build. And to preserve it without risk, for generations to come.

2

The Hazard of Unprotected Wealth

As currently structured, the tax system in this country levies an estate tax of up to 55%, with minimal deductions, on monies passed down from one generation to the next. There is no plan in sight for lessening this insidious erosion of your assets through multigenerational estate taxation. In fact, if anything, the government is considering decreasing the allowable exemptions and thereby depleting your estate even further.

If your estate is worth $50 million, after taxes your children will inherit only $22.5 million. And your grandchildren will only receive $10,125,000 after the estate taxes are deducted from the remainder. In only two generations, everything you have worked so hard to earn and protect will be depleted by almost 80%. One generation after that, only $4,556,250 will remain. And while $4,556,250 sounds like a nice inheritance, it cannot begin to compare with the $50 million with which you began.

Obviously, we are not taking into consideration the fact that your children could increase your estate substantially through their own investments and income. Should this occur, the numbers will change — although any increase in the estate value will be subject to the same or higher percentages of taxation.

Conversely, there is always the possibility that your children may come to decrease the value of the estate they inherit through poor investment, medical emergency, national economic down-swings, or by living an exorbitant lifestyle. In that case, they will pay a lesser amount of tax on a lesser amount of money.

No one can foresee what the economic future may bring. So for the purposes of this book, we are going to freeze your estate at its current value. The examples are still quite valid in that they represent the steady course of your estate as it flows through the generations of taxation.

With that aside, let us look at the ravages of taxation another way. Let's assume, to make things easier, that we live in a world of 10% interest. Even though the true numbers are currently a little less, the drama of this example remains evident. If your estate is worth $50 million and is earning a 10% rate of return, you are earning $5 million income a year. After income taxes of approximately one third, you have left a net yearly income of $3.3 million.

When you die and your estate passes to your children, they will earn $2,250,000 interest income on the $22.5 million they inherit. After they pay income taxes, they will be left with $1.5 million in yearly income. By the time your estate passes to your grandchildren, their $10,125,000 will produce $1,012,500 before taxes and only $675,000 of income per year — a far cry from the $3.3 million with which you started. And when you consider that these funds probably will be further diluted due to being spread between many children and grandchildren, you can see that even $50 million is not enough to preserve a financially secure future for your descendants if it is unprotected from the encroachment of estate tax costs.

Clearly, if $50 million is not sufficient to insure financial security for future generations, $10 million, which may seem like a tidy inheritance, will provide even less security after it suffers similar depletion.

Ten million dollars currently producing $1 million before income taxes and $666,000 after income taxes becomes about half, or $5 million, after estate taxes. In turn, that $5 million will produce $500,000 before income taxes and $300,000 after income to be shared by all your children. Your grandchildren will all share an inheritance of only $2.5 million from your original estate. This will generate approximately $250,000 before income taxes and $166,000 after income taxes, based on current assumptions. The security you thought you had provided is quickly dissipated as your grandchildren are left with only 20% of your original estate — the missing 80% has been given to the government in just two generations.

Bleak as this picture seems, it can get even worse.

Even if your estate is worth $10 million, it is probably not all liquid. Chances are you have some money in property and investments. Nonetheless, estate taxes are due on the total value of your entire estate within nine months. If your family does not have $5 million immediately available in cash to pay your estate taxes, they may have to liquidate assets and by doing so could suffer a significant additional loss. The other remedy to the situation is for them to borrow the money, but then they must pay interest on the borrowed amount, which will also represent a significant loss in their inheritance.

This chain of events is analogous to buying a house for $1 million. Over 15 years of paying the mortgage interest on this purchase, the cost of that house can double. So if your estate taxes are 50% of your $10 million estate — $5 million — and you must borrow the money to pay them, the finance charges you pay on the $5 million loan can actually double the tax costs to $10 million by the time you have paid them off. This means you have, effectively, paid your entire estate value in taxes.

In summation, if you are worth $10 million, when you die your estate taxes can be:

1. Paid with cash, in which case there will be $5 million in estate taxes, leaving only a $5 million inheritance.

2. Paid by liquidating assets for which you may get less than their true value. This could mean that your estate could be devalued and become worth only $7 or $8 mil-

lion, while remaining liable for the full tax amount of 50% — leaving only $3.5 or $4 million for your heirs.

3. Paid by your borrowing some or all of the $5 million required for estate taxes. Allowing for interest payments, this actually might cost $10 million, effectively leaving your children nothing to inherit.

But there is a fourth way to pay the estate tax costs. And, astonishingly, this fourth way will allow you to cover all the estate tax costs of your $10 million estate for only $500,000 to $1 million — that's 10 to 20 cents on the dollar — and it's completely guaranteed, based on current assumptions!

I'm going to tell you about that fourth way in the chapters to come. But before I do, I want to make sure that you understand the true implications of unprotected wealth. The list on page 24 outlines the shrinkage of estates of famous people. Pages 25–27 illustrate three specific cases of what can happen when estate tax costs are not properly provided for in estate financial planning. I show you these particular examples because the men involved were well-known personalities with substantial wealth. Though they all were prominent financial figures, none comprehended the importance of protecting his estate. Consequently, each estate was significantly reduced by estate taxes. Thus even respected and knowledgeable professionals from other seemingly related fields may not be qualified to understand or advise on matters of estate protection.

Estates of Famous Persons

NAME	GROSS ESTATE	SETTLEMENT COSTS	NET ESTATE	PERCENT SHRINKAGE
Stan Laurel	$ 91,562	$ 8,381	$ 83,181	9%
William Frawley	92,446	45,814	46,632	49%
"Gabby" Hayes	111,327	21,963	89,364	20%
Hedda Hopper	472,661	165,982	306,679	35%
Nelson Eddy	472,715	109,990	362,725	23%
Marilyn Monroe	819,176	448,750	370,426	55%
W.C. Fields	884,680	329,793	554,887	37%
Humphrey Bogart	910,146	274,234	635,912	30%
Dixie Crosby	1,332,571	781,953	550,618	59%
Erle Stanley Gardner	1,795,092	636,705	1,158,387	35%
Franklin D. Roosevelt	1,940,999	574,867	1,366,132	30%
Clark Gable	2,806,526	1,101,038	1,705,488	30%
Cecil B. DeMille	4,043,607	1,396,064	2,647,543	35%
Al Jolson	4,385,143	1,349,066	3,036,077	31%
Gary Cooper	4,984,985	1,530,454	3,454,531	31%
Henry J. Kaiser, Sr.	5,597,772	2,488,364	3,109,408	44%
Harry M. Warner	8,946,618	2,308,444	6,638,174	26%
Elvis Presley	10,165,434	7,374,635	2,790,799	73%
Alwin C. Ernst, CPA	12,642,431	7,124,112	5,518,319	56%
J.P. Morgan	17,121,482	11,893,691	5,227,791	69%
William E. Boeing	22,386,158	10,589,748	11,796,410	47%
Walt Disney	23,004,851	6,811,943	16,192,908	30%
John D. Rockefeller, Sr.	26,905,182	17,124,988	9,780,194	64%
Frederick Vanderbilt	76,838,530	42,846,112	33,992,418	56%

Your Estate Research Service © 1990 Longman Group USA, Inc.

Alwin C. Ernst
Founder and Senior Partner,
Ernst & Ernst, Accountants,
Cleveland, Ohio

56% Shrinkage

Gross Estate	$ 12,642,431
Total Costs	7,124,112
Net Estate	$ 5,518,319

Settlement Costs

Debts	$ 6,232
Administration Expense	58,862
Attorney's Fee	10,000
Executor's Fee	10,000
California Estate Tax	1,226,737
*Federal Estate Tax	5,812,281
Total Costs	$ 7,124,112

*No Marital deduction.

J.P. Morgan
Chairman of the Board,
J.P. Morgan & Co.,
New York, New York

69% Shrinkage

Gross Estate	$ 17,121,482
Total Costs	11,893,691
Net Estate	$ 5,227,791

Settlement Costs

Debts	$ 581,673
Administration Expense	182,332
Attorney's Fee	1,165,963
Executor's Fee	515,000
New York Estate Tax	2,064,414
*Federal Estate Tax	7,384,309
Total Costs	$ 11,893,691

*No Marital deduction.

Your Estate Research Service © 1990 Longman Group USA, Inc.

Conrad N. Hilton
Owner of Hilton Hotel Chain,
Santa Monica, California

53% Shrinkage

Gross Estate	$ 199,070,700
Total Costs	105,782,217
Net Estate	$ 93,288,483

Settlement Costs

Debts	$ 4,412,278
Funeral Expense	5,624
Attorney's Fee	399,418
Executor's Fee	399,418
California Estate Tax	156,819
*Federal Estate Tax	100,408,660
Total Costs	$ 105,782,217

*No Marital deduction. $9,494,845 in charitable bequests.

Your Estate Research Service © 1990 Longman Group USA, Inc.

3

Wealth Creation and Preservation

The need for estate tax cost protection and the devastation that occurs without it should now be painfully clear. And if I told you that there was an investment opportunity, stock, bond, or municipal fund available that would provide this protection at a guaranteed rate of return sufficient to reduce your estate taxes by up to 90% — and that it would pay its guaranteed return the very next day if required — you would clamor for the details and be eager to participate. Unfortunately no such investment, stock, bond, or muni exists. But I have promised you that there is a way to accomplish this financial miracle, and indeed there is. One way, and one way only — through life insurance.

For one reason or another, many of you may draw back at the mention of life insurance. Perhaps you've been advised against it by experts in other fields who don't fully comprehend the wondrous uses it offers. Perhaps you don't understand the tremendous leverage and tax advantage it represents. Perhaps you were once turned off by an overzealous insurance salesperson or an unknowledgeable stockbroker. Or maybe in the past you didn't want to face the fact of your own mortality. It doesn't matter. The bottom line is that, properly used, life insurance represents a guaranteed investment with returns from 2 to 1 to as high as 40 to 1, and it can be income and estate tax free! In other words, based on current assumptions, for each dollar given to an insurance company, the return can be as high as $40. Of course the actual return amount will vary based on your age, health, method of insurance and the carrier(s) you choose. But for the average older person, $1 million could easily produce a $10 million tax free return.

In a comparable situation, you would have to make over a $32 million profit on your investments or business—which would produce $21 million after income taxes — to result in approximately $10 million after estate taxes. Our concept requires only $1 million to produce the same $10 million in money that is income and estate tax free. In other words, $1 million does the work of $32 million.

Suppose I told you that I was with the Internal Revenue Service and for today only we are offering a special on estate tax rates that will effectively reduce your taxes by 90%. Furthermore, if you will give me $3 million today, I will give you a receipt that shows you to have paid the entire tax on your $50 million estate (based on current assumptions). At any other time, those taxes will equal $27.5 million, but for today you can pay them for only 10% of that amount. Wouldn't you rush to take advantage of this incredible offer? You would have to wait in line.

The IRS does not make this offer. But, in effect, the same end result can be accomplished by an insurance company using our wealth creation and preservation concept.

Think about it in terms of our earlier example: If your estate is worth $50 million, we've already shown you that 55% of your net worth will be lost to estate taxes when you die, leaving your heirs to inherit a sadly reduced amount. Life insurance can reduce the amount of that loss to only 10%.

If you and your wife purchase a Last-To-Die type of life insurance policy where for $2,750,000 both people are insured and the proceeds are paid upon the second death, your heirs can receive, based on your averaged age of 60, a return of $27.5

million — 10 times your investment — *tax free* upon your death.
So while the government still takes its 55% share of your
estate — $27.5 million — your family receives that same amount
back from the life insurance company that insured you. Your
estate passes on to your heirs virtually intact. In essence, you
have paid the total amount of your estate tax with only the
$2,750,000 cost of the life insurance policy — thereby effectively
reducing that tax cost to only 10% of what it would otherwise
have been, based on current assumptions. The bottom line is,
either your children will pay the entire amount in the future or
you can pay it now — at a 90% discount.

Remember, all of this was accomplished using only 5% of
your total estate value. Fully 95% remains available for you to
invest, spend, or use as you see fit. Of your original $50 million
estate, $47,250,000 remains for you to use in making an even
greater fortune. Meanwhile, a mere 5% — $2,750,000 — pro-
vides a guarantee of financial security for your heirs and your
posterity, whether it is needed tomorrow or 25 years from now.
Perhaps even more important, you know you have made one
more excellent investment and have further diversified your
portfolio.

The next step is for your heirs to do the same thing. They
purchase a life insurance policy on the estate they have inherited from you, now worth $47,250,000 ($50 million, less the
$2,750,000 cost of your original policy) as opposed to the $22.5
million they would have otherwise inherited. Their 55% tax liability means that, without insurance, their estate tax will be
$27.5 million, leaving only $22.5 million of your original $50 mil-
lion for your grandchildren to inherit. But with the insurance
they will save 90% of that tax liability. Assuming they have now
reached an averaged age of 60, for $2,598,750 they can purchase
$25,987,500 worth of insurance, which will cover their estate
tax costs. Your original $50 million estate passes to your grand-
children at $44,651,250 ($50 million, less the $2,750,000 cost of
your insurance and less the $2,598,750 cost of your children's
insurance), as opposed to the vastly depleted sum of

$10,125,000, which represents the unprotected amount of your estate after two generations of estate tax costs. This is a difference of an additional $34,526,250.

Often an accountant or other financial planner will refer to an internal rate of return when establishing the value of a given financial program. But you cannot really apply that concept to this approach because you do not know if you will die tomorrow, five years from now, or 30 years from now. An internal rate of return is a means of calculating time into the return on an investment. But to do so you must make certain assumptions, one of which concerns the amount of time over which the investment will mature to its full potential. But you are never guaranteed that you'll survive long enough to realize what may be considered a significant rate of return. What if you die tomorrow?

We had one major client with substantial insurance who died recently within six months of his purchase. The internal rate of return means nothing to him now. It's an uncomfortable thought, but unfortunately the possibility always exists. The investment you made that has not had time to mature will be worth approximately its original amount, while the life insurance policy you purchased will realize its full potential immediately. To compare an investment that offers a higher internal rate of return over time to a life insurance policy that guarantees its substantial return immediately, should it be needed, is to compare apples to oranges — the same conditions simply aren't being considered.

Let's look at it again from the standpoint of a $10 million estate.

With an estate of $10 million, you can expect to pay 50% in estate taxes. But with a guaranteed 10 to 1 return on an investment in a life insurance policy, based on current assumptions, you can pay the total $5 million tax assessment using only $500,000. At age 60, that $500,000 will purchase a policy worth $5 million. Once again, in effect, the life insurance company pays the taxes on your estate for a cost to you of 10 cents on the dollar.

These are simplified examples, yet they are completely accurate. There are many variables that will determine exactly how much insurance you need to buy and what kind of return you can expect to receive. At younger ages, it is possible to structure a policy that will provide a 20 to 1 return, meaning that in the case of the $50 million estate, enough insurance can be purchased to pay the tax liability of $27.5 million for only $1,125,000 — that's only five cents on the dollar!

In summary, properly purchased life insurance policies can:

- effectively discount estate taxes up to 90%;
- allow you to effectively avoid paying estate taxes on up to the first $20 million of your estate;
- effectively increase your $600,000 estate tax exemption manyfold;
- reduce your 55% estate tax bracket to 10% or less;
- pay your taxes at 10 to 30 cents on the dollar — better than any government flower bond in the past.

There is simply no other money-management vehicle available anywhere that offers such phenomenal benefits and rates of return when they are necessary. *This is truly the only means by which you can effectively preserve your estate intact for your children and grandchildren and protect the lifetime of hard work and dreams that your estate represents.* The actual event (death) that causes the need (taxes) produces the necessary money (life insurance) at the time it is needed.

In the rest of this book, we are going to take a more in-depth look at some of the specific variables and applications that this remarkable program affords. While some of the material may seem complex, just remember that it all comes back to this same basic plan: using life insurance to protect your estate from the ravages of estate taxation and to create and preserve great wealth for your children, grandchildren, and future generations.

4

Explore the Alternatives: Maximizing Estate Tax Cost Discounts

Now that we have examined the hazards of leaving your estate unprotected from estate taxation and have explained how life insurance can fully preserve wealth against those taxes, we will take a quick look at some of the types of policies available to accomplish these estate planning goals.

There are four basic types of policies: *Whole Life, Interest Sensitive Life, Universal Life,* and *Term Life.* Each has a distinct purpose and each fulfills a unique need in the marketplace.

WHOLE LIFE

Whole Life, sometimes called "Permanent Insurance," is a very traditional form of insurance policy that has existed for many years. Whole Life is designed to help consumers handle the high cost of insurance in later years, when premiums become prohibitively expensive, by averaging out premium costs and amortizing them over the projected lifetime of the policy. In this way, the high cost of later payments is transferred to earlier premiums, producing a leveling effect.

In most cases, Whole Life insurance policies include dividends, and those dividends are projected at a certain nonguaranteed rate each year.

As you pay the Whole Life insurance premiums, you will build up cash value in excess of the actual insurance costs. This excess is invested and the return on the invested portion is added back into your policy in the form of dividends. These dividends can then be used to limit the ongoing payment period of the policy.

INTEREST SENSITIVE LIFE

An Interest Sensitive policy is a type of Whole Life policy that pays a flexible interest rate. With a policy of this type, financial data is composed each year. Then the actual investment yield — based on the insurance company's portfolio — is calculated minus the insurance company's current mortality and operating expenses and an acceptable margin of profit.

The difference is passed on to the policyholder in the form of additional interest and cash value buildup.

UNIVERSAL LIFE

Universal Life is another form of Whole Life policy. It functions the same as Interest Sensitive insurance in terms of interest returns. However, it differs from Interest Sensitive Life in the way in which its premiums are paid.

While the Interest Sensitive policy requires that you adhere to a fixed-premium payment, Universal Life affords much greater flexibility. It allows you to make payments as you choose and in accordance with your cash flow. This presents a greater danger, however, because if you don't keep to a prescribed schedule you could discover one day that you do not have enough money in the policy to support the required death benefit. For this reason I prefer the Interest Sensitive policy, although in times of decreasing interest rates Whole Life may end up being the best of the three.

Universal Life has one great advantage. It will provide the

option of purchasing more insurance at first at no additional cost. This will allow you to accommodate any further growth of your assets without regard for future medical problems and at your current age.

In any event, no single type of policy is the best — proper analysis after looking at 10 or 20 companies (as shown on our charts on page 154) will tell you which company has the best policy for you. And whether it's called Whole Life or Interest Sensitive Life or Universal Life is completely irrelevant; whichever policy makes the most sense in your particular situation will become self-evident. In any event, you may use a variety of policies from various companies to give you the best diversified portfolio with the most flexibility.

TERM LIFE

There is one other form of life insurance policy available: Term Life insurance.

Many people are aware of Term Insurance and bought it when they were younger because it offered substantial benefits at a low cost — but only for a short period of time, while the insured was still young and healthy. As its name suggests, Term Insurance is only beneficial for short-term uses. If, for example, you were engaged in a business venture with someone and that venture was going to require two years to come to a profitable fruition, you might insure that person with Term Insurance for the two-year period to cut the risk factor of your endeavor. However, the cost of Term Insurance is determined by the mortality rate of the insured's age group, and the premiums increase each year, becoming extremely costly as the years go by. Thus, Term Insurance is not prudent for someone who has to keep insurance for the rest of his or her life, which is the case in estate tax discount planning.

There are many purposes that are wonderfully served by

Term Insurance, but estate tax planning absolutely is not one of them.

Sometimes limited amounts of Term Insurance are purchased as part of a total package. This serves as an option to cover additional needs that may arise as an estate appreciates or increases from inflation. Unfortunately, there are insurance agents and financial planners out in the marketplace today who are not familiar enough with the long-term benefits of insurance as a means to offset estate tax costs. These people may advise you to consider Term Insurance because of the initial perceived savings. They will show you, using tables and graphs, how much cheaper the same death benefit coverage is when purchased as Term Life. And they will be right — for a short period of time. But if you follow the numbers through the years, you will see quite clearly that no amount of initial savings can offset the long-term benefits of reducing your estate tax costs on a guaranteed basis. Furthermore, by the time you realize that your Term Insurance costs are far in excess of what you can reasonably afford — and what you could have been paying for some type of Whole Life policy — you will find even the costs of Whole Life prohibitive.

5

How to Achieve
the Greatest Discount

The insurance industry is one of actuarial tables and statistics. Several variables will determine exactly what death benefits you qualify for and at what price. These include your age, sex, and health. Policies can be bought on a male, female or on both lives; the latter is called a Last-To-Die, Survivorship or Second-To-Die policy.

According to statistics, women live longer than men. In addition, in most marriages the woman is younger than the man. So when the time comes for a couple to purchase insurance and plan for the continued financial security of their children and grandchildren, the woman represents a better risk to the insurance company and can get a better rate.

But there are times when it is better to insure the man. Perhaps the woman is uninsurable due to her age or health, or perhaps this is a second marriage and both partners have children by previous unions. If the man wants the children he has fathered to inherit his estate, it may be necessary for him to leave it to them directly rather than having it pass through his second wife. This could create an immediate need for insurance to pay estate taxes upon her death. The same applies to a woman if she is leaving money to her children from a former marriage. In any of these cases, it would be wise for each partner to purchase a separate Male or Female policy.

But if the woman is insurable and there are no reasons why a couple's estates should be kept separate, insurance used for estate tax discount purposes is as effective when taken out on the wife as when taken out on the husband — and generally less expensive.

In 1981, Congress passed the Unlimited Marital Deduction provision, which allows an estate of any size to pass from one spouse to the other with no estate taxes being levied. Only when the money passes outside of the marital situation are taxes collected. By insuring the woman, who is statistically more likely to live longer, the insurance company assumes it will have a longer period of time in which to collect interest on the premium payments. Therefore, since it will make more money over time, it can charge less for the policy. And because the insurance benefit will not be needed until both parents have died and the children are faced with the burden of estate taxes, this is generally the best way to proceed.

In some cases I will recommend one of the newest types of policies, called Last-To-Die. Since for estate planning purposes you don't need the death benefit money until both the man and woman have passed away (remember, the Unlimited Marital Deduction means no estate taxes will be paid as long as the money is passed to the spouse), a Last-To-Die policy that basically insures both the man and woman can be purchased. The combined survivorship of the two people will be greater than either one of them individually, so a longer period of time will pass before the policy pays off. The insurance company collects more premiums and earns the investment return on the premium payments longer. In these instances, we will find that the Last-To-Die policy offers the lowest premiums and the most efficient way of handling estate tax situations.

But what happens when both the man and woman are uninsurable due to age or health condition? Must they lose the bulk of their estate to taxation? Thankfully, no. Their children can use the same means to reclaim the estate within a single generation.

In this case, the grandparents gift their grandchildren with a sum of money. If there is a gift tax to be paid, they pay it, knowing it will still be less than the ultimate cost of leaving their estate unprotected. The grandchildren use the gift to purchase life insurance on the combined lives of their parents and, because their parents are still relatively quite young, the Last-To-Die policy produces a dramatic return. When the grandparents die, their children will lose up to 55% of their estate to taxation. But, one generation later, when the inevitable occurs and the grandparents' son and daughter-in-law pass away, the grandchildren will receive a life insurance benefit payment equal to the estate tax cost of the original estate. Although estate taxes were paid by the children on the estate of their parents and by the grandchildren on the estate they inherited from their parents, both amounts can be recovered in full and the estate now passes on to future generations recovered and almost fully intact.

The specifics of your situation will dictate which type of policy is best to accomplish your estate planning goals. *It is absolutely crucial that your policy be put together by a qualified, trained expert in this specific field or you could lose millions of dollars in death benefits for your estate.*

To fully comprehend the dramatic difference between levels of qualification, let's consider a male nonsmoker applying for $1 million of insurance. At age 30, the cost to this man for that $1 million of coverage in one payment is $30,844, based on current assumptions. Ten years later, when he is 40 years old, that same One-Pay insurance will cost him $59,378 — almost twice as much. When he is 60 it will come to $195,360 on a One-Pay basis, and at age 70 the cost will be $301,000.

As I explained earlier, if the insured is a woman, the rates are lower. For a 30-year-old nonsmoking woman, the cost for $1 million of insurance is $26,412 if she pays it in one payment. That cost is $43,060 when she is 40 — a significantly smaller increase than her male counterpart's. When she is 60 the cost is $140,656, and when she is 70 it is $253,000.

Obviously, the status of the applicant's health will have a similar effect on his or her qualification and cost level.

Let us look at another example of how this works: David and Kathy Smith have an estate worth $20 million. They need $10 million of life insurance to cover their estate tax costs or their children will inherit less than half of their original worth. Based on current assumptions, a life insurance policy taken out on David alone will cost $2,038,893 and will yield a 5 to 1 return.

Kathy Smith fits the insurance industry standards and is considered to be six years younger than David in terms of mortality plus her actual 3 years' age difference. The cost of a policy to insure Kathy alone for that same $10 million would be $1,471,668, which represents a 6.8 to 1 return.

However, if we were to insure both David and Kathy with a Last-To-Die policy that doesn't pay until both parties are deceased, the return jumps to 8 to 1. Now only $1,245,862 is needed for the same $10 million in paying the estate tax cost, which effectively discounts that tax cost by 88%.

Properly purchased, the difference between a Male, Female, or Last-To-Die policy can mean a difference of up to $793,031 — or an 8% difference in your estate tax cost discount.

The chart that follows outlines the Smith's options in purchasing a $10 million life insurance policy. The bottom half of the chart reflects the costs of financing the various policies over a period of six or seven years.

David & Kathy Smith
$10,000,000 Death Benefit

INSURED	OUTLAY	RETURN	ESTATE TAX DISCOUNT
David Smith	$ 2,038,893	5 to 1	80%
Kathy Smith	1,471,668	6.8 to 1	86%
David & Kathy	1,245,862	8 to 1	88%

Financed Method

INSURED	ANNUAL OUTLAY	NUMBER OF YEARS	TOTAL OUTLAY
David Smith	$ 419,825	6	$ 2,518,950
Kathy Smith	304,023	6	1,824,138
David & Kathy	220,875	6.4	1,415,084

Age

David Smith 64
Kathy Smith 61

All figures based on current assumptions

Return Per Dollar
What Each Dollar Paid to Insurance Company Produces at Death

AGE	MALE ONE PAY	FEMALE ONE PAY	LAST-TO-DIE	ESTATE TAX DISCOUNT
30	32 to 1	38 to 1	54 to 1	= 98%
40	19 to 1	32 to 1	44 to 1	= 98%
50	10 to 1	14 to 1	22 to 1	= 95%
55	7.5 to 1	10.7 to 1	15 to 1	= 93%
60	5.7 to 1	8.1 to 1	10.7 to 1	= 91%
65	4.4 to 1	6 to 1	7.8 to 1	= 87%
70	3.3 to 1	4.5 to 1	5.6 to 1	= 82%
75	2.8 to 1	3.3 to 1	4 to 1	= 75%
80	2.2 to 1	2.4 to 1	3.4 to 1	= 70%

All figures based on current assumptions

$100,000 of Premium
Buys These Death Benefits

AGE	MALE ONE PAY	FEMALE ONE PAY	LAST-TO-DIE		ESTATE TAX DISCOUNT
30	$ 3,200,000	$ 3,800,000	$ 5,400,000	=	98%
40	1,900,000	2,300,000	4,400,000	=	98%
50	1,000,000	1,400,000	2,200,000	=	95%
55	750,000	1,070,000	1,500,000	=	93%
60	570,000	810,000	1,070,000	=	91%
65	440,000	600,000	780,000	=	87%
70	330,000	450,000	560,000	=	82%
75	280,000	330,000	400,000	=	75%
80	220,000	240,000	340,000	=	70%

All figures based on current assumptions

$1,000,000 of Premium
Buys These Death Benefits

AGE	MALE ONE PAY	FEMALE ONE PAY	LAST-TO-DIE		ESTATE TAX DISCOUNT
30	$ 32,000,000	$ 38,000,000	$ 54,000,000	=	98%
40	19,000,000	23,000,000	44,000,000	=	98%
50	10,000,000	14,000,000	22,000,000	=	95%
55	7,500,000	10,700,000	15,000,000	=	93%
60	5,700,000	8,100,000	10,700,000	=	91%
65	4,400,000	6,000,000	7,800,000	=	87%
70	3,300,000	4,500,000	5,600,000	=	82%
75	2,800,000	3,300,000	4,000,000	=	75%
80	2,200,000	2,400,000	3,400,000	=	70%

All figures based on current assumptions

6

The "Right" Approach

The means by which insurance companies determine the cost of their policies is quite complicated. They must factor in mortality rates, death benefits, administration costs, profit, and interest income earned on both premium payments and cash value accumulation. Based on these elements, they set the cost of your premium payments. Obviously, if you pay the cost over time, another factor is introduced to the equation: the cost of financing the policy until there are no more premiums.

However, the factors on which the initial costs are determined do not remain constant. Changes in interest rates or mortality statistics, for example, will impact the insurer's original assumptions and projections. Therefore the insurance companies must reserve the right to adjust your payments or your premium-paying period over the life of your policy or overcharge to accommodate these changing factors.

Once the best type of policy (or policies) to apply to a specific situation is determined, the real future cost of that policy depends on the chosen insurance company's or companies' actual results rather than the original assumptions. The cost is determined by the actuarial and statistical results and by the fluctuating interest rate that the insurance company will earn on your premium dollars.

The means of payment are flexible. Different payment options fulfill different estate planning goals, and, to some extent, you can choose the amount of the premiums you want to pay and how long you want to pay them, depending upon your own cash flow.

One fact is obvious: The fewer payments you use to pay off your policy, the cheaper that policy will be. But there are occasions when paying off the entire policy is prohibitive or ill-advised. Although in the long run it may be cheaper to pay it off more quickly, your cash flow situation and your ability to continue to enjoy a satisfactory quality of life must be key elements in the evaluation of your plan and your decision-making process.

There are three basic means of paying off your insurance policy: One Pay; Limited Pay, which can also be called a Natural or Selected Vanish; and Lifetime Pay. Let us take a brief look at how each payment method works and what its advantages and disadvantages may be.

ONE PAY

A One Pay insurance policy is basically a discounted Limited Pay. The insurance company calculates the total amount of what your premiums would be if you paid them over a period of time and how much your extra financing costs would be. It then discounts your policy by that financing amount if you pay the entire cost in one immediate payment. Of course, the policy cost is still based on the then-current assumptions, and it is possible that sometime later, should assumptions change, additional premiums could be required. However, those additional premiums will be charged whether you paid over time or all at once, so you may as well at least benefit from the One Pay savings on the discounting of the future premiums if the cash flow is available.

LIMITED PAY

With a Limited Pay insurance policy, the premium is paid for a selected number of years. This could be five to eight years or even longer, until enough cash value is established to carry the policy. If it is more desirable, payments of 10 to 15 years can be arranged. After the selected payment period, the premium is considered to have "naturally vanished" and your payment schedule is complete. However, there is always a caveat (or condition) to the policy, which states that the premium may reappear based on changing mortality and interest rates.

LIFETIME PAY

You can select to pay your policy premiums over your lifetime. The insurance company uses its actuarial tables to determine your life expectancy. It then projects your payments over that period of time, adding in the extra amounts to cover its loss of interest income on the money not yet paid up front. This affords you the lowest cash flow impairment resulting in the lowest yearly premiums. You are still fully insured, however, and the entire amount of the policy benefit will be paid to your heirs immediately upon death regardless of what method of payment you use.

The drawback to this type of policy is obvious; the total cost over your lifetime can be many times in excess of what it might have been had you paid it off sooner. The advantage, of course, is that this type of payment option permits a lower cash flow cost each year, and for some people that could be important in maintaining their desired lifestyle.

CHOOSING AMONG THE POLICIES

Let us take a look at what the differences in these three types of payment options can mean.

If your estate is worth $20 million, you will need approximately $10 million to offset the cost of your estate taxes in order to preserve your estate intact for your heirs. Let's assume you are 50 years old and in good health, and the insurance company you have chosen is paying a 10% interest rate on your insurance, based on current assumptions. The cost of enough insurance to protect your estate will be only $1 million.

If you pay for that insurance in one payment, you will pay $1 million. This represents the present value of six discounted premiums. If you spread the cost out over six years, the total cost will be approximately $1.2 million. You have spent $200,000 more than you had to for the same amount of coverage.

How do you decide if you should make one payment?

The primary consideration is simple: Do you have the money? Can you afford to put it all up front — and do you want to? A lot of people simply like to be paid off and not have to worry about it. Even though there is always the possibility of assumptions changing and additional premiums being required, they like not having to remember or think about making their premium payments all the time.

Other people, despite being able to afford to make one total payment, prefer to keep their assets more liquid or to limit their exposure. Some of them even liken the decision to playing the odds. With the possibility that they might die the next day, they question why they should pay the whole premium when a single payment will guarantee the policy.

In response to this question, some insurance companies provide a larger death benefit in the earlier years to compensate for the additional premiums paid if death occurs prematurely.

Still others figure it out mathematically. They calculate the savings against the possible uses of the money to determine the true savings. Based on most of the current assumptions, you are getting the equivalent of an 8.25% tax free return on your money when you pay your insurance policy off in one payment. So if over the next five years you could make more than 8.25% tax free yearly or after taxes on that same money, then it would be to your advantage not to pay the insurance company the entire sum.

As an example, there was a man on the East Coast who was buying a rather large policy, and it was suggested that he make the payments over six years rather than in one large expenditure. He turned to his comptroller and said, "Don't we have a $20 million Certificate of Deposit right now?" The comptroller said, "Yes." He said, "What are we making on that investment?" and was told that the CD was currently earning 8% gross; after income tax, it netted about a 5% return. The man then decided to pay the entire $4 million policy cost up front because he preferred the 8.25% return of the discounted policy payments over the 5% return on the CD.

The question comes down to whether you have the cash flow, are psychologically disposed to taking care of the cost all at once (based on current assumptions), and can achieve any better rate of return on the money.

One final note. People ask what happens if they die during the first years of the policy when they have effectively overpaid for the length of time during which they were covered. One of two things generally occurs should this situation arise: Either the insurance company returns the overpayment amount (unused premiums), or the insurer pays more to the heirs using the amount they had been overpaid to determine an increased level of death benefits.

There is one additional reason *not* to use a One Pay policy. It is technically complicated, but has to do with a new tax law that became effective June 1988. Since that date, if you buy an insurance policy using a One Pay approach the policy is called a Modified Endowment. If, at some time in the future, your children (or the Irrevocable Trust you have established) want to borrow money against the value of the policy, that loan will be deemed to be on the LIFO (Last In, First Out) method of accounting. This means any money borrowed will be deemed to be earned interest first as opposed to the principal. And, as interest income, it will be subject to income tax.

However, if you pay your premiums over five, six, or seven years, you don't have this problem. In most Limited Pay situations, loans against the policy are considered to be principal and therefore are not subject to income tax.

Some people choose the One Pay plan expressly because it makes it prohibitive for the children or Trust to borrow against it. They do not want the money they have provided to discount their estate taxes to be squandered before it is really needed. Others like to keep the option open and opt for Limited Pay even though it will ultimately cost them more.

Only one thing is certain: Each buyer must be given all the pertinent information and then left to make a choice based on what is of greatest importance to him or her — there is no universal right way.

SINGLE PREMIUM

There are many people who bought Single Premium life insurance policies over the last few years. These policies generated tax free income through a loan procedure, but since the tax laws changed in June 1988, that tax free income is no longer available on policies issued after that date.

These policies placed all the emphasis on the tax free income; the death benefit itself was of only secondary importance. As a result, there was a lower initial death benefit. Yet many of the people who purchased these policies have never borrowed against them. They are not taking advantage of the tax free income (which, for those who bought before the June 1988 changes, were "grandfathered" so that they keep the benefit), nor will their estates benefit by any substantial amount upon their premature deaths. It might be very advisable for these people to look at the substantially increased immediate death benefit they could receive by either transferring from their current Single Premium policy to a new One Pay policy, or by taking the tax free loan money from the Single Premium policy and using it to buy additional coverage. In effect, it can be a method of paying for much-needed insurance with pretax dollars.

These policies can be changed on a tax free basis in accordance with Internal Revenue Code section 1035. This is an exchange of like properties for the purpose of deferring a taxable gain on the initial policy. This exchange can be affected from one life insurance policy to another or to an annuity. However, you cannot exchange an annuity for a life insurance policy. The new policy must be on the same insured as the old. Due to certain technicalities involved in the process you should consult a professional before completing an exchange of policies. Caution should be exercised and professional analysis utilized before any purchase changes are effected, because the excellent "grandfathered" tax-shelter advantages of the existing policies are no longer available.

There is a way to purchase a new policy using the tax free income from the Single Premium policy while still retaining the old Single Premium policy itself. To do so, simply borrow against your Single Premium policy using the tax free income to pay the premium on the new policy. In this manner you are optimizing your coverage utilizing pretax dollars. Comparisons of Single Premium policies versus One Payment policies are shown for a male age 70, 60, and 50 on the following pages.

Single Premium vs. One Payment
Male Age 70

PREMIUM TYPE	OUTLAY	DEATH BENEFIT	TAX FREE INTEREST RETURN
Single Premium	$ 1,000,000	$ 1,571,170	8.75%
One Pay Premium	1,000,000	3,342,000	7.50% Average after 5th Year

Single Premium Emphasizes
Tax Free Income

vs.

One Payment Premium Emphasizes
Tax Free Death Benefit Asset

All figures based on current assumptions

Single Premium vs. One Payment
Male Age 60

PREMIUM TYPE	OUTLAY	DEATH BENEFIT	TAX FREE INTEREST RETURN
Single Premium	$ 1,000,000	$ 1,436,782	8.75%
One Pay Premium	1,000,000	5,823,100	6.10% Average after 4th Year

Single Premium Emphasizes
Tax Free Income

vs.

One Payment Premium Emphasizes
Tax Free Death Benefit Asset

All figures based on current assumptions

Single Premium vs. One Payment
Male Age 50

PREMIUM TYPE	OUTLAY	DEATH BENEFIT	TAX FREE INTEREST RETURN
Single Premium	$ 1,000,000	$ 1,855,288	8.75%
One Pay Premium	1,000,000	10,024,400	6.30% Average after 4th Year

Single Premium Emphasizes
Tax Free Income

vs.

One Payment Premium Emphasizes
Tax Free Death Benefit Asset

All figures based on current assumptions

7

Better Protection
Through Diversification

Generally within the insurance industry, when an agent or broker is underwriting for a client he or she will have that client examined by the company that he or she represents or feels to be the best for that client's needs. But experience has convinced me that this is not the best procedure, and I now recommend that each person be examined by three or four insurance carriers in order to determine which one has the best policy for the client's specific health status. Interestingly, not all insurance companies treat the same health factors in the same way. Some consider certain health problems to be more severe than others, and their concern is reflected in the prices they quote. A recent example of this sometimes dramatic difference can be found in the story of a man who needed a $1 million insurance policy to offset the taxes on his $3 million estate.

The least expensive company that I showed him produced a health-based rating that made that company more costly than the highest priced firm. Another company with which he examined came back with a health rating far better than the first — they were willing to overlook certain conditions that the first company was not — and so, although they had appeared to be a much more expensive company on paper, in reality the insurance they offered became the most reasonably priced, once the ratings were done.

One client repeatedly called me after having applied for his life insurance. He was very concerned about his health and was buying a substantial policy of approximately $5 million. These calls continued for three and a half months during the difficult stage of medical underwriting. He persisted in calling on a daily and then weekly basis, asking if we were finished with our underwriting so he could pay for the policy and know that it was now in effect. Finally the day arrived that the insurance was completed. He called and I enthusiastically proclaimed that he was now insured and could immediately drop dead. He was greatly relieved.

This humorous story underscores a serious point: Purchasing life insurance is not simple and can, in fact, become quite complicated. Various doctors and hospitals must be contacted and financial reports summoned in order to consummate a policy. The insurance company must be convinced that there is an insurable interest as well as a legitimate need for the coverage amount, so that a person is not worth more dead than alive. The investigation that follows your signing an application is normal, and you can expect numerous interviews and time delays. Insurance is paid for by money, but it must be purchased with good health and appropriate need.

By examining with more than one company, then, you have a better opportunity to receive the best coverage at the best price. You should also be aware that no number quoted to you by any insurance salesperson is correct until you have been examined and the insurance companies have offered a price based on the findings of that examination.

It used to be that after examining for three, four, or even five companies, a person would choose the one that offered the best rate and use them to issue the needed coverage. But there is a far better and more prudent course of action that promises both a good rate and better long-term protection. Just as you would not put all of your investment dollars into one stock or bond no matter how secure and guaranteed it seemed but would, instead, diversify your portfolio, diversification of your insurance portfolio has also come to be the wisest way to protect your estate assets.

Traditionally, in cases where $20 million, $30 million, $50 million or more is needed by an estate to provide the coverage for discounting the estate tax costs, more than one insurance company had to be used because of the limited capacity individual carriers have to supply these extremely large amounts of coverage. Even the largest life insurer in the nation is limited to $20 million of coverage on their own. But even in cases where coverage amounts are lower, diversifying your portfolio is the most prudent, conservative, and advisable choice. Because insurance company rates are *based on current assumptions* and may change as those assumptions change, there is no way that one quote can offer the best overall price on a permanent basis. These changes in assumptions are not consistent from company to company, and increases in costs will not occur unilaterally across the industry. So the company that offers the best rate today will not necessarily offer the best rate tomorrow. By using more than one carrier, you will almost certainly be guaranteed the best long-term average rate available and will also enjoy the safety of using more than one company.

There is another reason why diversifying your insurance coverage is a wise course of action. Earlier in this book I explained that the guaranteed nature of the insurance "investment" is based both on the current assumptions used to quote rates of return and on the overall solvency of the company carrying your policy. I have always recommended that my clients use only substantial and reputable firms to provide their needed coverage, but nothing is guaranteed; as we have been seeing recently, even the largest, most reputable firms can suffer setbacks. With so much involved in terms of your estate planning, it is clearly prudent not to put all your eggs in one basket.

This idea of diversification of life insurance coverage is a very recent one, and many agents still fail to understand the increased leverage, safety, flexibility and average price protection it offers. Nonetheless, it is irrefutable that the strongest portfo lios are well diversified and include policies from several reputable firms, all represented by one common agent so that they can be properly administered.

One recent client needed $38.5 million to discount the taxes on his $70 million estate. He was examined by five companies and issued quotes based on the findings of those examinations. We took the four best firms and had him purchase $4 million with one company, $10 million with another, and split the remaining $24.5 million between the other two companies. In this way, his price was averaged and his portfolio protected through diversification. For this man, the immediate cost of his insurance, while impor-tant, was not the sole consideration. At his estate level, a few dol-lars one way or the other could not possibly matter more than the peace of mind and increased protection diversification offered. Even so, since all the companies were working on current assumptions and projections, he will undoubtedly benefit by hav-ing the best average cost in the long term.

The average savings, protection, and peace of mind this approach affords are not limited only to the extremely rich. The overall benefits of this new approach are so remarkable that it is advisable for clients at the $1 million or $2 million level as well as for those at the $50 million or $100 million level.

8

The Irrevocable Trust

Chances are that many of you reading this book to learn how to preserve your estate have already created a Living Trust. This is a Revocable Trust that can be changed at any time during your life. A Living Trust is a wise investment; in addition to allowing you to avoid probate costs, it will protect the privacy of your assets and is a method of structuring the current $600,000 per-person estate tax exemptions so that there will be no estate tax for the combined $1.2 million on a couple's estate.

It works like this: A husband and wife are setting up their estate and are considering how best to handle the $600,000 tax-exempt portions they are each entitled to pass on to their heirs. Assuming that the man will die first, if his $600,000 goes directly to his wife, it will become part of her estate and will be liable for estate taxes upon her death. Only her single $600,000 exemption will remain untaxed when her estate passes to their children. If it goes directly to the children, they will not pay estate tax on it but it will be beyond the wife's control or access. If, however, the man's $600,000 is placed in a Living Trust and structured properly, his wife will still have access to it and to the interest it will earn each year, but it will not be considered a part of her estate upon her death and therefore the children will inherit both the father's and the mother's $600,000 — a total of $1.2 million — estate tax free.

The problem with the Living Trust is that many people are under the impression that structuring their estates this way will prevent estate taxes being levied on far greater amounts than just the $1.2 million of their combined $600,000 exemptions. This is simply not true. The Living Trust only protects that first $1.2 million from estate taxes. Even if all of the man's money was in the Living Trust upon his death, and his wife then died and the money went to the heirs, they must still pay the full estate tax on all but the $600,000 exemption from each of their parents.

So as a tool to be utilized in protecting your estate from depletion by taxation, a Living Trust is only useful up to $1.2 million. Anything above that amount will still suffer the full ravages of estate taxes at levels as high as 55%. It will be 60% from $10 million to $21,040,000.

How, then, can this couple protect their heirs' financial security and avoid the decimation of their estate by taxes? One method is through an Irrevocable Trust, which differs from a Living Trust in that all the monies held within it are estate tax free.

There are many reasons why a couple, when considering their estate planning, might not wish for the principal of their estate to pass directly to their children. Perhaps the children are minors or are physically or mentally disabled. Or perhaps the couple wants to insure that the principal will continue to pass untouched to their grandchildren and great-grandchildren. Yet they still want their children to have full use of the interest income earned on their estate without having to suffer the loss incurred by estate taxation. By establishing an Irrevocable Trust, they can accomplish exactly that.

An Irrevocable Trust is a financial entity that exists outside the estate of the couple. Money that they put into it during their lifetimes will remain free of estate taxation upon their deaths. Whereas monies in a Living Trust would pass to the heirs upon the death of the person in whose name the Trust had been established and would then be taxed, monies in an Irrevocable Trust remain within the Trust and are not taxed. The heirs may use the income the Trust generates (they will pay full income tax on any money the Trust earns), but the principal remains intact and untaxed through the generations.

Knowing this, we can now use the leverage of life insurance purchased through the Trust to protect the full value of the Trust from estate taxation.

The estate of Mr. and Mrs. Taylor is worth $10 million, and they want to see to it that the full amount passes on to their children and grandchildren. They want their children to live off the income but not to be able to spend the principal. To guarantee this, they establish an Irrevocable Trust. (See appendix for sample irrevocable trust.) But they can't put all their money into the Trust while they are alive, because they need it to live on. And when they die, as their money passes from them into the Trust, it will be taxed. Their children will lose half the estate and thus will have only the interest from $5 million — roughly $500,000, based upon 10% interest — a year to live on as opposed to $1 million, the income on their original $10 million estate.

To prevent this, Mr. and Mrs. Taylor put $500,000 into the Irrevocable Trust. They can afford this much out of their estate without it adversely affecting their lifestyle. And there is no gift tax to be paid, since the amount falls within their combined $1.2 million exemption. With that money, the Trust purchases a life insurance policy on them worth $5 million.

When the Taylors die, the $5 million of insurance death benefit comes to the Trust estate and income tax free. And although the government has taken 50% of their original $10 million, the remaining $5 million also goes into the Trust. Now the Trust has the full $10 million and the estate continues through the generations at its full value, with the children and grandchildren living comfortably on the $1 million income earned by the principal each year.

The amazing leverage of life insurance combined with the tax advantages of using an Irrevocable Trust to avoid income and estate taxes on that life insurance is outstanding in preserving the assets that took you a lifetime to build.

9

Compounding Your Wealth

I have spoken throughout this book of the incredible leverage life insurance offers as a means of discounting estate taxes in order to preserve financial security for future generations. But the power of life insurance in estate planning can extend even further. It can actually contribute not only to preserving wealth but also to creating it.

Thanks to what is often referred to as "The Miracle of Compound Interest," the savings that an estate enjoys as a result of using life insurance to reduce estate tax costs can multiply significantly. In only two generations–50 years–the savings can become worth many times more than the original investment.

We have already seen that, if your estate is worth $10 million, your estate tax cost will be $5 million and your heirs will be left with the interest earnings of the remaining $5 million on which to live. We also know that by using life insurance to discount your estate taxes, you can provide your heirs with almost the full $10 million less only the cost of the insurance policy itself.

Without the protection the life insurance offers, your heirs would augment their own finances nicely with the added income your $5 million estate afforded them. And it is very possible that they may not actually need the additional income the increased estate will provide. In other words, they may not need the income generated by the full estate value in order to lead financially secure lives.

However, the following charts will show you some astonishing information. They will demonstrate what can happen when the interest income generated by the savings you enjoy on your estate tax costs is allowed to compound over a period of 50 years. This represents the statistical life expectancy of grandchildren following the death of their grandparents. Remember, this is "found" money—money your estate would not have if it weren't for your purchase of life insurance to preserve your full estate value from the cost of estate taxation. By leaving only the portion of your estate which represents this "extra" money to compound annually, your heirs and their heirs can create ever greater wealth for all your posterity to enjoy.

The means by which this occurs is quite simple: Money is transferred to an Irrevocable Trust. Life insurance is purchased by the Trust. There will be no gift tax on the money transferred to the Trust as long as the amount is within your Unified Gift and Estate Tax Exemption ($600,000 each for a man and his wife). If it is structured properly, you can also use your yearly $10,000 gift exemptions ($20,000 combined for a man and his wife) for as many family members as you wish the money to go to. As discussed earlier, since the death benefit that the Trust will receive upon your death is insurance proceeds, it is income tax free, and since it is outside your estate, it is not subject to any estate tax. The heirs can either take a yearly return based on those savings or can allow those savings to compound over a lifetime. Based upon an assumption of 10%, the principal amount left in the compounding savings account of the Trust will double approximately every 10 years based on a 7% net after-tax return within the Trust. *So in 50 years the interest earned on a principal amount of $4 million ($5 million in saved estate tax cost less $1 million cost of insurance based upon age 60) will compound to be worth $120,229,584!*

Think of it...money that they would not otherwise have had

at all can generate incredible wealth in only two generations, virtually without effort or risk. All thanks to the miracle of compound interest (see pages 69–70).

Of course, the exact amount of tax savings and, therefore, interest income potential will be determined by the amount of your estate, your age, the cost of your insurance, and the savings you are able to enjoy. Interest rates paid by savings institutions will also effect earnings. The charts on pages 65–68 assume a 10% interest rate — 7% net after income taxes–which is currently common. Though this is subject to change, it will serve as a perfectly fine example of how dramatic the wealth creation can be.

The four charts show the interest income earning potential of estates from $1 million to $200 million and are broken down into age and gender brackets of female age 50, male age 60, male age 70, and female age 80. The specifics of your situation will determine the exact amount your estate can earn, but these charts will serve as guidance in helping you to establish your long-range estate planning goals.

In column one you will see the estate size and in column two the amount of the federal estate tax cost on each estate. Column three shows the cost of a One Pay life insurance policy based on that specific age which, based upon current assumptions, would effectively pay the estate taxes. Column four depicts the resulting savings to the estate achieved by the discounted estate tax; it is the total tax cost (which is the same as the insurance policy) minus the cost of the policy. In column five you will see the annual 7% net return after income taxes (10% gross interest before taxes) on those savings in perpetuity. In the sixth column the yearly interest income from column five is shown after having been compounded for a 50-year period. This period represents the approximate life expectancy of the insured's grandchildren after his death.

These charts reflect the startling results of the savings accomplished by using the wealth creation and preservation methods outlined in this book.

Female Age 50

1 ESTATE SIZE	2 FEDERAL ESTATE TAX	3 INSURANCE COST	4 SAVINGS TO ESTATE	5 ANNUAL 7% NET RETURN (1)	6 SAVINGS COMPOUNDED AT 7% - 50 YEARS (1-2)
$ 1,000,000	$ 153,000	$ 11,208	$ 141,792	$ 9,925	$ 4,177,205
3,000,000	1,098,000	79,109	1,018,891	71,322	30,013,933
5,000,000	2,198,000	158,147	2,039,853	142,790	60,088,436
10,000,000	4,948,000	355,742	4,592,258	321,458	135,274,694
20,000,000	10,948,000	786,858	10,161,142	711,280	299,317,450
25,000,000	13,750,000	988,189	12,761,811	893,327	375,925,421
50,000,000	27,500,000	1,976,163	25,523,837	1,786,669	751,856,741
75,000,000	41,250,000	2,964,138	38,285,862	2,680,010	1,127,788,031
100,000,000	55,000,000	3,952,112	51,047,888	3,573,352	1,503,719,351
200,000,000	110,000,000	7,905,940	102,094,060	7,146,582	3,007,387,719

(1) Net after tax
(2) Grandchild estimated to live 50 years after death of grandparents

All figures are based on current assumptions.

Male Age 60

1	2	3	4	5	6
ESTATE SIZE	FEDERAL ESTATE TAX	INSURANCE COST	SAVINGS TO ESTATE	ANNUAL 7% NET RETURN (1)	SAVINGS COMPOUNDED AT 7% - 50 YEARS (1-2)
$ 1,000,000	$ 153,000	$ 27,033	$ 125,967	$ 8,818	$ 3,710,613
3,000,000	1,098,000	192,470	905,530	63,387	26,674,220
5,000,000	2,198,000	385,043	1,812,957	126,907	53,404,320
10,000,000	4,948,000	866,475	4,081,525	285,707	120,229,584
20,000,000	10,948,000	1,916,873	9,031,127	632,179	266,030,134
25,000,000	13,750,000	2,407,409	11,342,591	793,981	334,118,987
50,000,000	27,500,000	4,814,571	22,935,429	1,605,480	675,609,507
75,000,000	41,250,000	7,221,732	34,028,268	2,381,979	1,002,371,543
100,000,000	55,000,000	9,628,894	45,371,106	3,175,977	1,336,497,807
200,000,000	110,000,000	19,230,654	90,769,346	6,353,854	2,673,794,900

(1) Net after Tax
(2) Grandchild estimated to live 50 years after death of grandparents

All figures are based on current assumptions.

Male Age 70

1	2	3	4	5	6
ESTATE SIZE	FEDERAL ESTATE TAX	INSURANCE COST	SAVINGS TO ESTATE	ANNUAL 7% NET RETURN (1)	SAVINGS COMPOUNDED AT 7% - 50 YEARS (1-2)
$ 1,000,000	$ 153,000	$ 46,583	$ 106,417	$ 7,449	$ 3,135,163
3,000,000	1,098,000	332,767	765,233	53,566	22,541,923
5,000,000	2,198,000	665,891	1,532,109	107,248	45,131,808
10,000,000	4,948,000	1,498,702	3,449,298	241,451	101,606,493
20,000,000	10,948,000	3,315,744	7,632,256	534,258	224,823,991
25,000,000	13,750,000	4,164,303	9,585,697	670,999	282,366,552
50,000,000	27,500,000	8,328,358	19,171,142	1,341,980	564,725,245
75,000,000	41,250,000	12,492,410	28,757,590	2,013,031	847,113,484
100,000,000	55,000,000	16,656,470	38,343,530	2,684,047	1,129,486,759
200,000,000	110,000,000	33,314,920	76,685,080	5,367,956	2,258,914,759

(1) Net after tax
(2) Grandchild estimated to live 50 years after death of grandparents

All figures are based on current assumptions.

Female Age 80

1 ESTATE SIZE	2 FEDERAL ESTATE TAX	3 INSURANCE COST	4 SAVINGS TO ESTATE	5 ANNUAL 7% NET RETURN (1)	6 SAVINGS COMPOUNDED AT 7% - 50 YEARS (1-2)
$ 1,000,000	$ 153,000	$ 64,640	$ 88,360	$ 6,185	$ 2,603,258
3,000,000	1,098,000	462,558	635,442	44,481	18,718,666
5,000,000	2,198,000	925,743	1,272,257	89,058	37,477,341
10,000,000	4,948,000	2,083,706	2,864,294	200,500	84,374,015
20,000,000	10,948,000	4,610,170	6,337,830	443,648	186,694,052
25,000,000	13,750,000	5,790,029	7,959,971	557,198	234,477,500
50,000,000	27,500,000	11,579,840	15,920,160	1,114,411	468,960,987
75,000,000	41,250,000	17,369,660	23,880,340	1,671,623	703,444,209
100,000,000	55,000,000	23,159,470	31,840,530	2,228,837	937,927,725
200,000,000	110,000,000	46,320,670	63,679,330	4,457,553	1,875,804,055

(1) Net after tax
(2) Grandchild estimated to live 50 years after death of grandparents

All figures are based on current assumptions.

Compound Interest Table

YEAR	CASH FLOW	COMPOUND VALUE AT 6.0%	COMPOUND VALUE AT 8.0%	COMPOUND VALUE AT 10.0%	COMPOUND VALUE AT 12.0%
1	$ 100,000	$ 106,000	$ 108,000	$ 110,000	$ 112,000
2	0	112,360	116,640	121,000	125,440
3	0	119,100	125,970	133,100	140,490
4	0	126,240	136,040	146,410	157,350
5	0	133,820	146,930	161,050	176,230
6	0	141,850	158,680	177,150	197,380
7	0	150,360	171,380	194,870	221,060
8	0	159,380	185,090	214,350	247,590
9	0	168,940	199,900	235,790	277,300
10	0	179,080	215,890	259,370	310,580
11	0	189,820	233,160	285,310	347,850
12	0	201,210	251,810	313,840	389,590
13	0	213,290	271,960	345,220	436,340
14	0	226,090	293,710	379,740	488,710
15	0	239,650	317,210	417,720	547,350
16	0	254,030	342,590	459,490	613,030
17	0	269,270	370,000	505,440	686,600
18	0	285,430	399,600	555,990	768,990
19	0	302,550	431,570	611,590	861,270
20	0	320,710	466,090	672,740	964,620
21	0	339,950	503,380	740,020	1,080,380
22	0	360,350	543,650	814,020	1,210,030
23	0	381,970	587,140	895,430	1,355,230
24	0	404,890	634,110	984,970	1,517,860
25	0	429,180	684,840	1,083,470	1,700,000

Compound Interest Table (*Cont.*)

YEAR	CASH FLOW	COMPOUND VALUE AT 6.0%	COMPOUND VALUE AT 8.0%	COMPOUND VALUE AT 10.0%	COMPOUND VALUE AT 12.0%
26	0	454,930	739,630	1,191,810	1,904,000
27	0	482,230	798,800	1,310,990	2,132,480
28	0	511,160	862,271	1,442,090	2,388,380
29	0	541,830	931,720	1,586,300	2,674,990
30	0	574,340	1,006,260	1,744,940	2,995,990
31	0	608,810	1,086,760	1,919,430	3,355,510
32	0	645,330	1,173,700	2,111,370	3,758,170
33	0	684,050	1,267,600	2,322,510	4,209,150
34	0	725,100	1,369,010	2,554,760	4,714,250
35	0	768,600	1,478,530	2,810,240	5,279,960
36	0	814,720	1,596,810	3,091,260	5,913,550
37	0	863,600	1,724,560	3,400,390	6,623,180
38	0	915,420	1,862,520	3,740,430	7,417,960
39	0	970,350	2,011,520	4,114,470	8,308,120
40	0	1,028,570	2,172,450	4,525,920	9,305,090
41	0	1,090,280	2,346,240	4,978,510	10,421,700
42	0	1,155,700	2,533,940	6,024,000	11,672,310
43	0	1,225,040	2,736,660	6,024,006	13,072.990
44	0	1,298,540	2,955,590	6,626,400	14,641,750
45	0	1,376,460	3,192,040	7,289,040	16,398,760
46	0	1,459,040	3,447,400	8,017,950	18,366,610
47	0	1,546,590	3,723,200	8,819,740	20,570,600
48	0	1,639,380	4,021,050	9,701,720	23,039,070
49	0	1,737,750	4,342,740	10,671,890	25,803,760
50	0	1,842,010	4,690,160	11,739,080	28,900,210

10

The Incredible Leverage
of Life Insurance for
Estate Tax Planning

U sing life insurance to create and preserve wealth by helping
to obviate estate tax losses is a simple concept. As you've
seen, however, some of the specifics that determine the best solu-
tion to any single situation can be very complex. Now that you are
more comfortable with some of the terms and planning theories
that define the program, you will be better able to truly comprehend the multitude of uses to which it can be put. The examples
that follow illustrate different solutions I have developed for a
variety of estate tax situations. The examples represent a cross
section of ages, estate sizes, estate tax situations, and tax discounts realized, some of which may be similar to your own current
position.

Facing each example is a pie chart that graphically depicts, in
the simplest manner possible, the remarkable leverage insurance
offers as a means of reducing estate tax costs. These pie charts
are exact duplicates of the ones we send to interested prospects
who have contacted us for advice. After they've completed an
information sheet that describes their financial status, we are
able to respond with a letter and chart showing the savings they
can expect. A copy of the information sheet is included here so
that you can see the exact process by which these cases were initiated and resolved.

71

CHART ONE

The first chart shows the $1 million estate of a husband and wife, both 53 years old. They require $153,000 to pay their estate tax cost. They can achieve a 94% discount on that cost by transferring $9,383 one time or $2,182 a year for five years to their children or an Irrevocable Trust, based on current assumptions. The Trust will purchase a Last-To-Die life insurance policy on the husband and wife. This will produce a 16.3 to 1 return of $153,000 upon the death of the last survivor and allow this couple's heirs to pay the taxes on their estate for about six cents on the dollar.

Chart 1

94% DISCOUNT
ON YOUR ESTATE TAX COST

$9,383 Transferred to Irrevocable Trust

Pays $153,000 Tax on Your $1,000,000 Estate

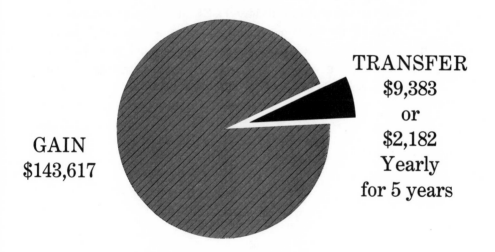

GAIN
$143,617

TRANSFER
$9,383
or
$2,182
Yearly
for 5 years

16.3 to 1 Return
$153,000

Prepared For: Mr. & Mrs. Client

Equal Age 53/53 $9,383 Deposit

Based on Current Assumptions
©1990 Barry Kaye Associates

CHART TWO

This chart shows a male age 64 with a $3 million estate. He has remarried but his wife has signed a prenuptial agreement. He wishes to leave his entire estate to his children from his first marriage. Therefore, since his estate will pass outside of the marital deduction, there will be estate taxes due within nine months after his death. That tax of $1,098,000 can be paid with a One Pay policy costing $241,967 based on current assumptions or a Limited Pay policy costing $48,843 a year for six years. This provides a 4.5 to 1 return and a 78% discount on his estate tax cost. It further effectively reduces his estate tax bracket from 55% to 8%.

He has separately purchased a $1 million life insurance policy on his life for the benefit of his second wife in order to accommodate her future needs. In order to conserve his cash flow, he is purchasing the new policy for his wife on a Lifetime Pay basis of approximately $25,000 a year.

Chart 2

78% DISCOUNT
ON YOUR ESTATE TAX COST

$241,967 Transferred to Irrevocable Trust

Pays $1,098,000 Tax on Your $3,000,000 Estate

TRANSFER
$241,967
or
$48,843
Yearly
for 6 years

GAIN
$856,033

4.5 to 1 Return
$1,098,000

Prepared For: Client

Male Age 64 $241,967 Deposit

Based on Current Assumptions
© 1990 Barry Kaye Associates

CHART THREE

Our third chart depicts a $5 million estate. The man is uninsurable and therefore we are utilizing his wife as the insured. She is 68 years old. He has chosen to pay the premiums over five years, based on current assumptions, at a rate of $100,581 yearly. He is gifting the funds to buy the insurance to an Irrevocable Trust and so places the payment sum in the Trust each year for it to pay the premium, instead of transferring a One Pay amount of $432,241 all at once. Ultimately, upon his wife's death, the Trust will receive approximately a 5.1 to 1 return of $2,198,000. This will pay the entire tax on his $5 million estate, effectively reducing his estate tax bracket from 55% to 9% and providing him with an 80% discount on his total estate tax cost.

Chart 3

80% DISCOUNT
ON YOUR ESTATE TAX COST

$432,241 Transferred to Irrevocable Trust

Pays $2,198,000 Tax on Your $5,000,000 Estate

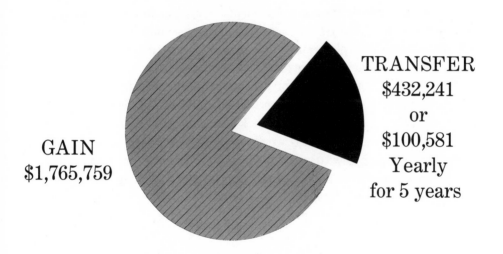

GAIN
$1,765,759

TRANSFER
$432,241
or
$100,581
Yearly
for 5 years

5.1 to 1 Return
$2,198,000

Prepared For: Client

Female Age 68 $432,241 Deposit

CHART FOUR

The fourth chart illustrates the $10 million estate of a man who is 67 years old and his wife who is 62 years old. They are taking advantage of the Unlimited Marital Deduction; therefore the tax of $4,948,000 on their estate value will not be due until after the death of the second spouse. They are considering transferring $568,130 either to their two children or to an Irrevocable Trust. After the gift is consummated, the children or the Trust will purchase a Last-To-Die life insurance policy with a payment amount of $4,948,000 to pay the taxes on the parents' $10 million estate. They can either transfer the entire $568,130 at this time or have the children or Trust pay for the policy over a five-year period at a rate of $132,123 yearly, based on current assumptions. Paid in one payment, this plan represents an 8.7 to 1 return and there will be no gift taxes, income taxes, or estate taxes.

The husband did not wish to utilize monies from his other assets or his investment portfolio to pay the insurance premium, so he went to the bank and took a mortgage against his unmortgaged home, which was worth approximately $2 million. He had enough cash flow to support the debt service. In this manner, his home, which would have been worth $2 million at his death, will now be worth $2 million less an approximate $600,000 loan amount for a net value of $1.4 million. However, the $5 million policy, at his death, effectively increases the net value of that house from $1.4 million to $6.4 million. He has produced the additional $5 million necessary to offset the estate taxes that will have to be paid by his family. He has put the plaster and walls of his house to work far beyond what their value would have been. In effect, he pays for the $5 million of insurance at a rate of approximately $66,000 interest a year (based on 11% interest), with the balance of the loan principal to be paid from the death proceeds.

They have effectively reduced their estate tax bracket from 55% to 6% and accomplished an 89% discount on their estate tax cost.

Chart 4

89% DISCOUNT
ON YOUR ESTATE TAX COST

$568,130 Transferred to Irrevocable Trust

Pays $4,948,000 Tax on Your $10,000,000 Estate

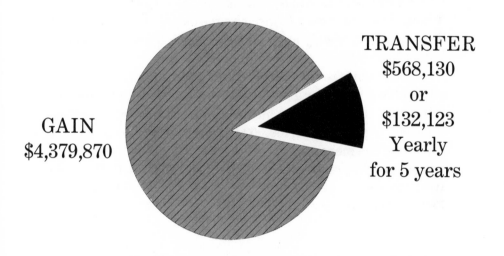

TRANSFER
$568,130
or
$132,123
Yearly
for 5 years

GAIN
$4,379,870

8.7 to 1 Return
$4,948,000

Prepared For: Mr. & Mrs. Client

Equal Age 67/62 $568,130 Deposit

Based on Current Assumptions
©1990 Barry Kaye Associates

CHART FIVE

The fifth chart shows a $25 million estate. Our client is a 59-year-old widower who now has both his estate and that of his deceased wife. He is anxious to accommodate the estate tax problem for his three children before his death. Since he lives in a community property state, he is further concerned with making these arrangements at the earliest convenience so that, should he remarry, his children will still be fully protected.

Even if he were to remarry, he could not take advantage of the Unlimited Marital Deduction because he wants to leave his money directly to his children, and therefore it will pass outside of the marital deduction upon his death and be subject to estate taxation. Thus the money to discount the estate taxes needs to be available immediately upon his death, and a policy must be purchased on his life.

He intends to transfer $2,306,038 to an Irrevocable Trust. He will pay whatever gift taxes are necessary at that time. The Trust will then purchase a life insurance policy on him, based on his age, to pay the $13,750,000 tax due upon his death. In this manner, the money will be received by the Trust income and estate tax free, representing a 6 to 1 return. This will effectively reduce his estate tax bracket from 55% to 10% and will produce an 83% discount on his estate tax cost.

Chart 5

83% DISCOUNT
ON YOUR ESTATE TAX COST

$2,306,038 Transferred to Irrevocable Trust

Pays $13,750,000 Tax on Your $25,000,000 Estate

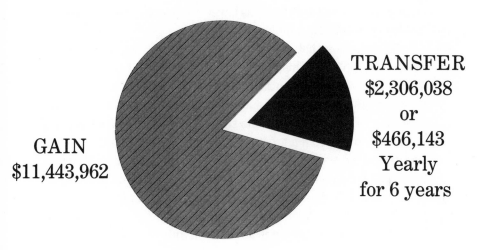

GAIN
$11,443,962

TRANSFER
$2,306,038
or
$466,143
Yearly
for 6 years

6 to 1 Return
$13,750,000

Prepared For: Client

Male Age 59 $2,306,038 Deposit

Based on Current Assumptions
© 1990 Barry Kaye Associates

CHART SIX

In the sixth chart we see an example of a widow, age 74, with a $50 million estate and ultimately a $27.5 million estate tax exposure. Her assets produce more than enough income for her standard of living and current lifestyle. She has been advised to transfer $7,849,280 to an Irrevocable Trust for the purchase of a One Pay life insurance policy, or $1,825,291 yearly for five years (based on current assumptions) for a Limited Pay policy that will, upon her death, produce enough money to cover the taxes. In this manner, she will receive a 71% discount on her estate tax cost. Since this will not change her lifestyle, she feels more comfortable paying the estate tax bill at this lower rate rather than having her children pay the $27.5 million at her death.

She realizes that she will have to pay gift taxes of approximately $3,765,104. This, coupled with the cost of the insurance itself, involves a total outlay of over $11.6 million, but she feels that that cost is far more acceptable than the $27.5 million alternative. She further understands that the gift taxes of $3,765,104 will be removed from her estate if she lives more than three years and therefore will further reduce the overall cost by approximately $1.9 million to $9.7 million. In effect, $9.7 million is buying $27.5 million. This is known as the three-year Contemplation of Death rule. The government says that if you pay a gift tax and die within three years, they will add it back into your assets.

Chart 6

71% DISCOUNT
ON YOUR ESTATE TAX COST

$7,849,280 Transferred to Irrevocable Trust

Pays $27,500,000 Tax on Your $50,000,000 Estate

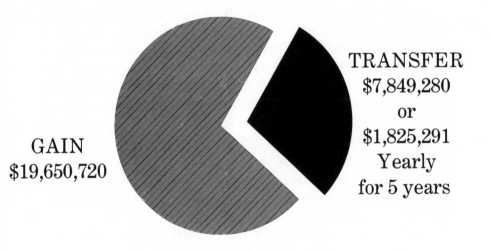

GAIN
$19,650,720

TRANSFER
$7,849,280
or
$1,825,291
Yearly
for 5 years

3.5 to 1 Return
$27,500,000

Prepared For: Client

Female Age 74 $7,849,280 Deposit

Based on Current Assumptions
© 1990 Barry Kaye Associates

CHART SEVEN

The seventh chart illustrates a $75 million estate belonging to a 79-year-old man and his wife, who is 71. They will accomplish a 78% discount on their estate tax cost by transferring $9,036,410 to an Irrevocable Trust. The Trust will then pay the $41,250,000 estate tax cost due upon their deaths with a life insurance policy purchased for that purpose. This represents a 4.6 to 1 return with a cost of $9,036,410 for them now, compared to $41,250,000 their children would otherwise lose upon their deaths.

This couple will probably pay for their policy over a five-year period, based on current assumptions, at the rate of $2,101,490 annually. Both the husband and wife can gift, tax exempt, $10,000 yearly to each of their four children and seven grand-children — a total of $220,000. They will pay gift taxes on all trans-fers in excess of this $220,000 yearly. However, they realize that the total cost of $10,507,450 for the Limited Pay life insurance policy plus the approximately $5 million in gift taxes (which would have been paid upon their deaths in any event and may save $2,750,000 for the estate) is still an extremely substantial savings over the $41,250,000 total tax cost without the discount.

The approximate savings their estate will realize — $32,213,590 — will produce a return, at 7% net after income taxes, of $2.1 million a year in perpetuity. Or, if left to compound over the 50-year life expectancy of their grandchildren after their own deaths, it will eventually produce an estate worth $883,710,752. This puts their One Pay $9,036,410 or $2,101,490 yearly outlay for five years into proper perspective as an excellent investment.

Chart 7

78% DISCOUNT
ON YOUR ESTATE TAX COST

$9,036,410 Transferred to Irrevocable Trust

Pays $41,250,000 Tax on Your $75,000,000 Estate

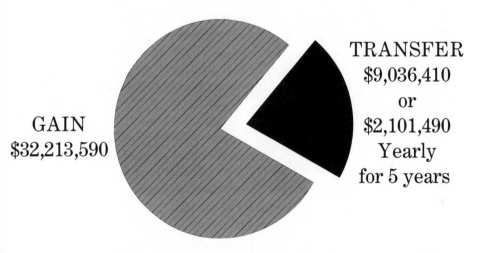

TRANSFER
$9,036,410
or
$2,101,490
Yearly
for 5 years

GAIN
$32,213,590

4.6 to 1 Return
$41,250,000

Prepared For: Mr. & Mrs. Client

Equal Age 79/71 $9,036,410 Deposit

CHART EIGHT

The eighth chart shows us a $100 million estate with an ultimate estate tax of $55 million. Our client is a divorced woman, age 60, with two children and one grandchild.

We have recommended that she transfer $6,769,630 to an Irrevocable Trust for the benefit of her family. The Trust will then purchase a $55 million life insurance policy on her life to pay the estate tax. This will represent an 8.1 to 1 return. Upon receipt of the $6,769,630 One Pay premium payment, based on current assumptions, the life insurance company will add the gain of $48,230,370 in order to produce the $55 million death benefit that will pay in full whether she dies tomorrow or 30 years from now.

The transfer and resulting gift taxes will still represent less than 10% of her total assets and will produce an 88% discount on her family's estate tax costs. She has effectively diversified her portfolio and still has 90% of her assets available (approximately $90 million) for her other investments and to support the lifestyle of her choice.

Chart 8

88% DISCOUNT
ON YOUR ESTATE TAX COST

$6,769,630 Transferred to Irrevocable Trust

Pays $55,000,000 Tax on Your $100,000,000 Estate

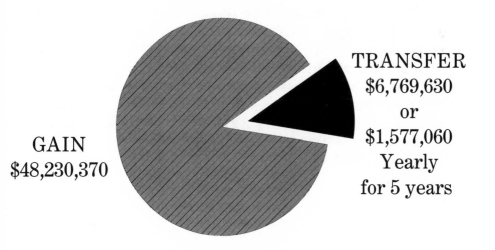

GAIN
$48,230,370

TRANSFER
$6,769,630
or
$1,577,060
Yearly
for 5 years

8.1 to 1 Return
$55,000,000

Prepared For: Client

Female Age 60 $6,769,630 Deposit

Based on Current Assumptions
©1990 Barry Kaye Associates

CHART NINE

The ninth chart shows a $200 million estate. This divorced man is 72 years old, and ultimately his heirs will have to pay $110 million in estate taxes. This figure represents the upper range of the maximum of insurance that can be purchased on one life. Naturally, a consortium of insurance companies would have to be used to accomplish this amount of death benefit.

He would transfer $37,308,930 to an Irrevocable Trust. The resulting insurance death benefit of $110 million to pay the tax would represent a 2.9 to 1 return. This is a lower than usual return because of his advanced age. However, it still provides a 66% discount on his estate tax cost and is superior to any flower bond approach used in the past. His gift taxes of over $20 million will bring the total cost to approximately $57 million (approximately $47 million net if he survives three years or more after the gift is made to the Irrevocable Trust). This still represents better than a 50% discount on his estate tax cost, effectively reducing his estate tax bracket from 55% to 25%, and leaves him over $150 million to work with during his lifetime, thereby not negatively impacting his lifestyle or investment programs.

Chart 9

<u>66% DISCOUNT</u>
ON YOUR ESTATE TAX COST

$37,308,930 Transferred to Irrevocable Trust

Pays $110,000,000 Tax on Your $200,000,000 Estate

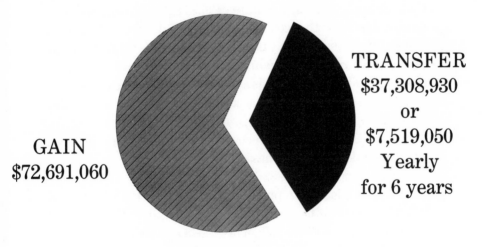

GAIN
$72,691,060

TRANSFER
$37,308,930
or
$7,519,050
Yearly
for 6 years

2.9 to 1 Return
$110,000,000

Prepared For: Client

Male Age 72 $37,308,930 Deposit

CHART TEN

The tenth chart shows a man worth in excess of $1 billion. His estate tax will be $275 million on each $500 million remaining in his estate at the time of his death. Since we cannot purchase more than approximately $100 million on any individual, we have chosen to insure various members of his family including himself. In this manner, there will be some money to pay the estate taxes at his death and additional monies coming back into the inherited estate at the time of future deaths to offset the initial taxes paid on each $500 million of his estate.

Insuring other family members allows us to work with younger ages, so it only requires $26,811,201 transferred to an Irrevocable Trust to accommodate a 10.3 to 1 return of $275 million to offset the estate taxes paid on each $500 million of his estate. (Naturally, once again, there will be gift taxes of approximately $7 million net upon his survival after three years.)

In this manner, he has accomplished approximately a 90% discount on his estate tax cost by assuring his grandchildren that they will ultimately receive recovery of the taxes paid at his death when his children, who he has also insured, die.

Most important, the $26,811,201 insurance cost plus gift tax costs of $7 million still represent less than 4% of his more than $1 billion in assets. If he can achieve a better return, through other investments, he still has 96% of his assets and $966 million available to achieve those results. This transfer guarantees a return on his investment, based on current assumptions, that will provide some liquidity immediately — tomorrow if need be — and a further diversification of his portfolio.

Chart 10

90% DISCOUNT
ON YOUR ESTATE TAX COST

$26,811,201 Transferred to Irrevocable Trust

Pays $275,000,000 Tax on Your $500,000,000 Estate

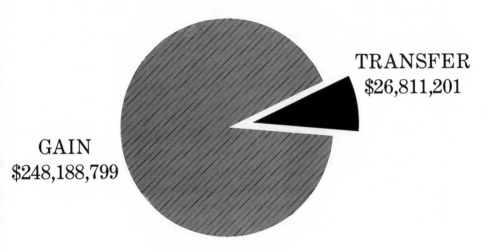

TRANSFER
$26,811,201

GAIN
$248,188,799

10.3 to 1 Return
$275,000,000

Prepared For: Clients

Ages 69-36 $26,811,201 Deposit

Based on Current Assumptions
©1990 Barry Kaye Associates

Summary of
Charts 1 through 10

CHART	AGE	DISCOUNT	NET ESTATE ASSETS	FEDERAL ESTATE TAX TAX	ONE PAYMENT INSURANCE COST	RETURN PER DOLLAR
1	53-53	94%	$ 1,000,000	$ 153,000	$ 9,383	16.3 to 1
2	M-64	78%	3,000,000	1,100,000	241,967	4.5 to 1
3	F-68	80%	5,000,000	2,200,000	432,241	5.1 to 1
4	67-62	89%	10,000,000	5,000,000	568,130	8.7 to 1
5	M-59	83%	25,000,000	13,750,000	2,306,038	6 to 1
6	F-74	71%	50,000,000	27,500,000	7,849,208	3.5 to 1
7	79-71	78%	75,000,000	41,200,000	9,036,410	4.6 to 1
8	F-60	88%	100,000,000	55,000,000	6,769,630	8.1 to 1
9	M-72	66%	200,000,000	110,000,000	37,308,930	2.9 to 1
10	69-39	90%	500,000,000	275,000,000	26,811,201	10.3 to 1

All figures based on current assumptions

"WEALTH CREATION and PRESERVATION"
Prospective Client Information Sheet

Source: _____ State: _____ Date of Lead: _____

Rep: _____ Occupation: _____ Retired From: _____

Name: _____ Date of Birth: _____

Spouse: _____ Date of Birth: _____

Address: _____

_____

Home Phone: _____ Business Phone: _____

# of Children: _____ # of Childrens' Spouses: _____

# of Grandchildren: _____

Your Health:	Your Spouse's Health:
Excellent ☐ Good ☐ Fair ☐ Poor ☐	Excellent ☐ Good ☐ Fair ☐ Poor ☐
Smoker ☐ Non-Smoker ☐	Smoker ☐ Non-Smoker ☐
Health Problems_____	Health Problems_____

Estimated Net Worth: _____ Estate Taxes (Death Benefit): _____

(Optional Information)

Assets: CDs _____   T-Bills _____   Munis _____

Stocks _____   Real Estate _____   Other _____

Remarks: _____

_____

FOR COMPANY USE

Illustrations: _____

Male OP ☐   Female OP ☐   Last-To-Die ☐

_____   _____   _____
Insurance Co.   Insurance Co.   Insurance Co.

02/89
(Revised)   **WEALTH CREATION CENTERS ■ BARRY KAYE ASSOCIATES**
1840 Century Park East, Suite #600, Los Angeles, CA 90067 (213) 277-9400 FAX (213) 282-0775

11

Creative Planning Techniques
Equal Tremendous Savings

How $150 Million Was Produced
at an Approximate Cost
of Only $6 Million

There are many other examples of how life insurance combined with Irrevocable Trusts, Living Trusts and Charitable Remainder Trusts (see Chapter 15) can be beneficial to an individual's particular situation. The following stories illustrate these approaches.

There is no limit to the creativity that can be applied once all the facts about a client's financial portfolio are known to the professional advisors. Many people are hesitant about revealing these facts; sadly this only penalizes their own families in the end. The more a financial advisor knows about a client's estate, the more he can apply various methods of wealth creation and preservation, thus arranging tremendous discounts and asset preservation. The following are a few of the programs I have been able to design to create $150 million at an approximate cost of only $6 million.

$15,000 YEARLY PAY AS YOU GO PLAN
PAYS $1.1 MILLION TAX
ON A $3 MILLION ESTATE

I am going to show you a simple concept that applies to any size estate. However, I will discuss a $3 million estate and the resulting estate tax of $1.1 million. Take the last $250,000 of that

$3 million that is effectively sitting in CDs or T-bills and you only use it to produce income of approximately $15,000 a year net after taxes. You never intend to invade that principal and effectively it is the "bottom" dollars of your principal. By transferring that $250,000 to an Irrevocable Trust and in turn to a life insurance company, based upon your age and current assumptions, your family will have $1.1 million available income and estate tax free to pay the taxes at your death.

What is your loss? What is your real effective cost?

The cost is the $15,000 a year income, the loss then is only $15,000 of extra income to spend each and every year. If you can afford to give up this $15,000 yearly, then in effect you have arranged to pay your $1.1 million estate taxes on your $3 million estate for only $15,000 yearly. And at death, there will be $1.1 million available income and estate tax free.

This is my Pay As You Go Plan, and it is a very inexpensive way to pay your estate taxes. Naturally, this concept can be applied to larger amounts, but it puts your cost of paying those taxes in proper perspective.

$5 MILLION PROTECTS THE PROCEEDS FROM A $100 MILLION GAIN

A leveraged buyout in Texas was to provide $100 million for the founder of a company. This represented great wealth creation. The stock brokerage firm involved asked if our wealth preservation techniques could be used to keep this $100 million estate intact for the man's family.

The brokerage firm was instructed to explain to their client that he had two options. He could take the full $100 million of the buyout, in which case he would suffer the pain of capital gains tax and, ultimately, estate tax. Or he could receive only $95 million from the buyout and in so doing provide for a complete recovery for his family of the $33 million of income tax and eventually $36 million of estate taxes. The cost for this recovery was only $5 million, with minimal income tax and gift tax at this time.

The $5 million would purchase approximately $69 million of life insurance based on current assumptions. This would replace all of the taxes ultimately paid as a result of the leveraged buyout of $100 million.

Obviously, he chose the $95 million and full tax recovery rather than the immediate $100 million.

$3.6 MILLION IN ESTATE TAXES PAID, PLUS $1,242,000 GIVEN TO CHARITY — ALL FOR ONLY $10,368 A YEAR TOTALLY OFFSET FOR THE FIRST 16 YEARS BY INCOME TAX SAVINGS

This is an actual case involving two clients of mine, Howard and Ruby. Howard and Ruby were worth approximately $8 million. Their federal estate tax was calculated to be about $3.6 million. A major part of Howard's estate was tied up in 10,000 shares of one company's stock, which he had received many years before in return for the purchase of his company. His cost basis was approximately $5 per share, and the stock was currently selling at $345 per share. This would mean that if he sold his stock prior to death, when he would receive a stepped-up cost basis, he would have to pay a substantial capital gains tax. At death the original cost basis is "stepped up" to the current market price, thus eliminating any income tax on the profit. The objective with this case was to diversify Howard's portfolio by allowing him to sell 3,600 shares, receive a stepped-up cost basis while he was alive, avoid paying capital gains tax, and pay the total estate taxes for his family — at a 100% discount. Howard also expressed an interest in leaving some of his estate to his favorite charities.

We were able to show Howard how he could accommodate every aspect of his desired program while still being able to leave over $1 million to his favorite charities — and all at a net cost to him of only $10,368 per year.

Here's how he does it:

1. Howard transfers the 3,600 shares of his $345 per share stock ($1,242,000) to a Charitable Remainder Trust.
2. The Trust sells the stock and pays no capital gains tax.
3. Howard receives a 10% annual (estimated) income of $124,160 for life.
4. Howard's after-tax return of $89,000 on the $124,160 income is transferred gift tax free to an Irrevocable Trust for the benefit of his children and grandchildren.
5. The Irrevocable Trust purchases a $3.6 million insurance policy on his wife Ruby's life for an annual premium of $89,000.
6. Upon Ruby's death, the proceeds of the life insurance of $3.6 million will be received by the Trust, income and estate tax free, to offset the $3.6 million estate tax to be paid on the $8 million estate.
7. Upon Ruby's death, the amount from the Charitable Remainder Trust, $1,242,000, will become the property of the charities specified.

By following this course, Howard and Ruby have met all of their objectives without sacrifice and without loss of their own financial security.

The Too-Often-Used Alternatives

If you are good to charity, Uncle Sam is good to you. If Howard had sold his 3,600 shares at the same price, $1,242,000, without the gift to charity, he would have had to pay a tax of $347,760. The net proceeds of $894,240 would still have been a part of his estate and ultimately would have been exposed to federal estate taxes of $491,832. His children would have been left with a net of $402,408 instead of the $3.6 million they received from the insurance to pay off all of the estate taxes. Furthermore, Howard and Ruby would not have received the satisfaction of giving substantial gifts to their favorite charities.

The end result is that Howard and Ruby have accomplished their objectives at a cost of only the loss of their annual $4 per share dividend on the 3,600 shares of stock that the Trust sold — a total of $10,368 per year net after income taxes. However, they have received an income tax deduction of approximately $422,280, which represents an immediate savings of $118,238 in income taxes — an amount that more than offsets the future losses of $10,368 per year for the next 16 years.

What Could Have Been

The only remaining point to discuss is what Howard's and Ruby's stock might have produced for the benefit of their family if it had not been sold and had remained in their estate. The chart below indicates the current price of $345 per share. Howard and Ruby believed the stock had the potential to reach $500 per share over the next decade. First we figured out what the stock might have produced using their $500 per share prediction. But then we took it even further and looked at what might occur if the stock were to go to $1,000 per share. To be fair — because the stock market does not produce a guaranteed result — we also looked at what might happen were the stock to drop to $200 per share.

In this manner, you can see what the total value of the 3,600 shares would have been at various levels and what the resulting federal estate taxes due upon their deaths would be. The final column shows the net after estate taxes, that is, the sum that would have been received by their children. This ranged from $324,000 to $1,620,000 without the insurance investment, versus the immediate income taxes and estate tax free amount of $3.6 million available at death made possible by utilizing the previously detailed wealth creation and preservation techniques.

At the bottom of this chart, you will see a figure of $2,222 per share. This is the amount to which the current $345 per share stock would have to increase in order to ultimately net for the children the same $3.6 million that they will have received using our program. However, they would not have received the immediate income tax savings of $118,238 and the charity would not have received a $1,242,000 gift. Also, what are the chances that the $345 per share stock will reach $2,222 per share? On the other hand, if it does, Howard and Ruby will still have 6,400 shares left.

Howard & Ruby Own 3,600 Shares of a Stock Selling at $345 a Share

Current

SHARE PRICE	TOTAL VALUE	FEDERAL ESTATE TAX	NET TO CHILDREN AFTER TAX
$ 345	$ 1,242,000	$ 683,100	$ 558,900

If Stock Price Goes To...

SHARE PRICE	TOTAL VALUE	FEDERAL ESTATE TAX	NET TO CHILDREN AFTER TAX
$ 200	$ 720,000	$ 396,000	$ 324,000
500	1,800,000	990,000	810,000
1,000	3,600,000	1,980,000	1,620,000
2,222	8,000,000	4,400,000	3,600,000

HOW TO TURN $269,262
INTO $750,000 A YEAR FOREVER

Chart A illustrates how one payment of $269,262, based on current assumptions, guarantees $750,000 yearly to be paid to this man's children and grandchildren in perpetuity after his death. In effect, 2.8 times his original outlay will be realized upon his death, each and every year in the future. This represents a 28 to 1 return. If changes in interest rates prevent the guaranteed payment, the insurance company will return his original $269,262 outlay plus a gain of $7,230,738 to the family at any time in the future after his death. This is based upon purchasing an insurance policy for $7.5 million at age 33. At his death, the insurance company actually pays $7.5 million, which is held at interest by the insurer, thus providing the yearly payments of $750,000, based on 10% interest. Since the principal is held by the insurance company, the family at any time can request a return of that principal, which would provide the initial outlay of $269,262 and the balance of $7,230,738 to make up the complete death benefit of $7.5 million. This is just another way of explaining the merits of the life insurance policy and what it can mean to an individual's family for many generations to come. It is certainly a prime example of substantial wealth creation.

Chart A

One Payment of $269,262 Guarantees $750,000 Yearly Forever Upon Death

2.8 Times Your Original Outlay Each Year

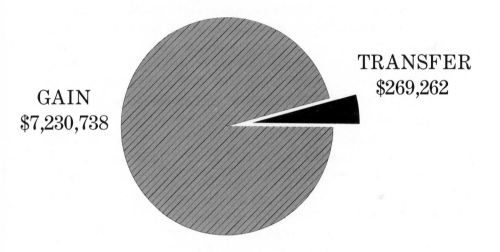

GAIN
$7,230,738

TRANSFER
$269,262

28 to 1 Return

If interest prevents guaranteed payment,
we will return your $269,262 outlay
plus a gain of $7,230,738

Prepared For: Client

Age 33

Based on Current Assumptions
©1990 Barry Kaye Associates

$13,750,000 RECOVERS THE ESTATE TAX ON $25 MILLION AT NO COST

In Chart B, the client and his wife are both 40 years old and his parents are both in their 80s, uninsurable due to age and poor health and not expected to live more than four years. The parents' estate is worth approximately $25 million, with a potential $13,750,000 in estate taxes. Our objective ultimately is to replace the entire $13,750,000 paid at the parents' death at no cost whatsoever to the client.

The parents transfer $1.5 million to an Irrevocable Trust now and pay $750,000 in gift taxes, which is the same that would have to be paid upon their deaths three to four years from now. In so doing, they have removed an extra $750,000 from the estate and from estate taxes, thereby ultimately saving the $375,000 that will be more than enough to pay for $13,750,000 worth of insurance on the son's and daughter-in-law's life for the benefit of the grandchildren.

When they pay the $311,120 One Pay premium, using part of the savings described above, it will have produced immediately on the death of the last survivor, based on current assumptions, $13,750,000 income and estate tax free. To equal these figures the parents would have had to produce $42 million from the $311,120 so that after income taxes it would be $28 million and after estate taxes it would be the same $13,750,000. Since they were in the manufacturing business and produced only a 10% return on sales, they would have had to make $420 million in sales to produce the $42 million in profit.

The $13,750,000 of savings will produce $1 million of income at 7% net for the family in perpetuity or, compounded over the remaining 50 years that the grandchildren are expected to live after their grandparents' death, will produce approximately $420 million. All for a cost of $311,120 — or if the grandparents live longer than three years, for nothing. Another example of the tax advantages and leverage of life insurance.

Chart B

98% DISCOUNT
ON YOUR ESTATE TAX COST

$311,120 Transferred to Irrevocable Trust

Pays $13,750,000 Tax on Your $25,000,000 Estate

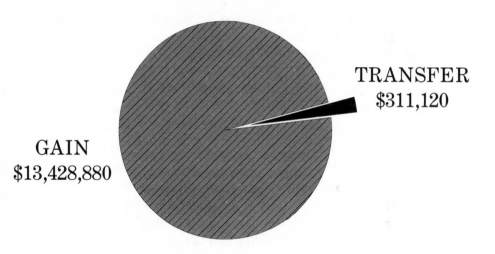

TRANSFER
$311,120

GAIN
$13,428,880

44 to 1 Return
$13,750,000

Prepared For: Mr. & Mrs. Client

Equal Age 40/40 $311,120 Deposit

Based on Current Assumptions
©1990 Barry Kaye Associates

$20 MILLION AT NO COST—THE SAME PREMIUM BUYS 3.3 TIMES MORE

A client on the East Coast had an estate exceeding $100 million and required $55 million of insurance to pay for his estate taxes at a 91% discount. A part of his program included already existing life insurance policies.

In many cases these policies can be optimized if to do so is in the best interest of the client. Sometimes, however, policies have become antiquated or were inferior protection at the time they were purchased. In other instances, a faulty technique has been implemented whereby the older husband's life is insured, rather than a combination of the husband and younger wife for a Last-To-Die type of policy. This type of plan produces a much lower premium, thus substantially optimizing the death benefit. In this particular situation, antiquated policies and the use of faulty techniques had produced $8,772,000 of insurance at a yearly premium of over $190,894. By changing these policies to the new Last-To-Die approach, we would be able to purchase $29,147,000 of insurance for the same yearly premium. This produced an extra $20 million of death benefit to offset the substantial taxes on this man's estate at no additional cost to him whatsoever. It provided 3.3 times the death benefit for the same premium.

The approximate $35 million balance of the client's insurance need was completed by utilizing additional insurance on him as well as his children to discount the estate taxes on his total $100 million estate and to accommodate the entire $55 million tax cost ultimately for the benefit of his grandchildren.

12

Optimize Your Exemptions

The magic $600,000 Unified Gift and Estate Tax Exemption. How can you optimize it? What can you do with it? Is it really the same upon your death as it is during your lifetime?

If you have the cash flow and it doesn't adversely affect your lifestyle, you can optimize this $600,000 and make it worth many, many times more. If you don't have the cash flow, you can still turn a smaller amount of money into the exempt $600,000.

MAKE $600,000 WORTH $360,000 A YEAR FOR LIFE

Let's begin by looking at how we can optimize the $600,000 exemption for your spouse at the time of your death. Remember, your Unified Gift and Estate Tax Exemption can be used either at your death as a credit against the taxes to be paid or during your lifetime to offset the gift taxes to be paid at that time.

Let's see what happens when one man utilizes the $600,000 during his lifetime and produces for his wife, at his death, $360,000 in yearly income. Another man waits until his death to use the exemption, at which time his wife receives the $600,000 in her Trust, from which she will receive a yearly income of $60,000.

Why the vast difference, and how can you be the spouse who receives $360,000 yearly?

We are going to make certain assumptions. We will assume that our client can afford to spend the extra $600,000 during his lifetime, and we'll assume that, at the time of his death, we are in a world of 10% interest. The first man takes the $600,000 from his estate and places it in a Trust for the benefit of his family. The Trust purchases a life insurance policy that pays a 6 to 1 return of $3.6 million upon his death, based on current assumptions. His wife has use of the income from the principal held in the Trust and receives approximately $360,000 a year in interest income for the rest of her life.

The second man did not have the cash flow to spend the $600,000 during his lifetime. His exemption passed to his wife at the time of his death and produces, at the same 10% rate, only $60,000 of interest income per year.

In both instances, the same $600,000 exemption was utilized. Obviously, then, if you have an extra $600,000 and it will not impact your lifestyle, it is better to gift the money during your lifetime rather than waiting until death. In this manner, you can significantly increase the income for your spouse, another example of substantial wealth creation.

"BUY" THE $600,000 EXEMPTION AT GREATLY REDUCED COST

In instances where there is a shortage of cash flow, we can actually purchase a $600,000 exemption by buying life insurance as indicated below. For example, if a man wished to transfer $600,000 to a Trust but also wanted to invest that money in real estate, he could accomplish both goals by purchasing a One Pay life insurance policy at age 60 for $103,255. This would provide $600,000 at his death at an 83% discount and would still leave $496,744 for the Trust to make other investments. If a female was age 55 and wanted to purchase the same $600,000 exemption, her One Pay life insurance policy would cost $63,368, based on current assumptions. This would provide her $600,000 at an 89% discount.

Once again, using the leverage of life insurance, allowable exemptions are maximized to provide the greatest possible return.

Your $600,000 Exemption Can Cost Only...

AGE	MALE	MALE DISCOUNT	FEMALE	FEMALE DISCOUNT
30	$ 18,437	97%	$ 15,809	97%
40	35,360	94%	25,726	96%
50	60,081	90%	42,432	93%
55	78,757	87%	63,368	89%
60	103,255	83%	83,498	86%
65	134,729	78%	111,133	81%
70	178,344	70%	129,997	78%
75	235,769	61%	178,832	70%
80	273,000	45%	250,000	42%

Why tie up $600,000 when your Unified Gift and Estate Tax exemption can be discounted?

All figures based on current assumptions

INCREASE YOUR $600,000
EXEMPTION SO YOU PAY NO TAXES ON
ESTATES OF UP TO $20 MILLION

On the chart that appears on page 109, you will see how the $600,000 exemptions can be maximized to cover the estate taxes on estates of up to $77.5 million! For example, a 40-year-old male can utilize his $600,000 exemption to purchase approximately $10 million of life insurance that ultimately would cover the estate tax on the first $18.8 million of his estate. In this manner, utilizing his $600,000 exemption, based on current assumptions, he will effectively pay no taxes on the entire gross taxable estate.

Similarly, a 55-year-old female will be able to use her exemption of $600,000 to purchase approximately $5.7 million of insurance to pay the estate taxes on the first $11.3 million of her estate.

Finally, a husband and wife who together are an average age of 65 will be able to use their combined exemptions of $1.2 million to purchase approximately $6.5 million to cover the total estate taxes on their $12.7 million estate, based on current assumptions.

Using this information, you can clearly see how you can effectively avoid paying taxes on a large taxable estate by utilizing your $600,000 exemptions and thus increasing the estate substantially.

Effectively Avoid Paying Estate Taxes
Increase Your $600,000 Exemption

Pay No Taxes on the Following
Gross Taxable Estate

AGE	MALE	FEMALE	HUSBAND & WIFE
30	$ 36,000,000	$ 41,500,000	$ 77,500,000
40	18,800,000	25,000,000	43,900,000
50	11,800,000	15,800,000	27,600,000
55	9,200,000	11,300,000	20,500,000
60	7,200,000	8,900,000	16,100,000
65	5,800,000	6,900,000	12,700,000
70	4,600,000	6,000,000	10,600,000
75	3,700,000	4,600,000	8,300,000
80	2,600,000	2,900,000	4,100,000

All figures based on current assumptions

13

The Leverage Keeps on Growing

INCREASE YOUR PENSION
FROM $1 MILLION TO $5 MILLION

Many of our clients have a considerable sum in their defined benefit, money purchase pension plan, KEOGH program or IRAs. These plans may recently have been frozen or rolled into an IRA. Distributions must be initiated by the time the participants are 70½ years old.

Let us assume that a $1 million IRA exists and that the income must be distributed starting at age 70½. Let us further assume that the client has no need for the income from this distribution and is only anxious to let the Pension Trust accumulate tax free income until his death.

Let's see what happens when the client dies with $1 million in the Trust. There is no stepped-up basis upon his death, so the income tax will reduce that asset to approximately $650,000 (depending upon his bracket and the state in which he lives). Then there will be the additional 55% estate tax, assuming his total assets are worth in excess of $3 million. And a further excise tax of up to 15% may also be charged, depending upon his situation. So the net result after all these taxes could be that less than $300,000 goes to his family.

This could have been avoided if he had terminated the plan and transferred the money to an Irrevocable Trust on a gift tax free basis. The Trust would then have bought a $5 million policy assuming his return was approximately 8 to 1, based on the charts shown in this book. His children would have received $5 million upon his death, income and estate tax free.

His pension assets would have to increase from $1 million to $17 million to equal the aforementioned $5 million after income and estate taxes. If his $1 million investment *could* increase to $17 million, after income and excise taxes it would be worth less than $10 million, and after federal estate taxes the net result to his children would be less than the $5 million we achieved utilizing the leverage of the wealth creation concepts.

In some instances, people have left substantial amounts to charity in their wills. One client optimized his gift by terminating his pension plan and gifting the entire $1 million to charity, thus offsetting any income taxes that would have been paid upon the termination of the plan. In turn, the $1 million purchased (based upon his age and his wife's age) for that charity $10 million of insurance. In this manner, he gave substantial money to charity ($10 million) in lieu of his children receiving, as described before, less than $300,000. This may also free up other assets in his estate which he originally had willed to charity and which now could go to his children.

Increase Your $1,000,000 Pension Plan to $5,000,000 Income & Estate Tax Free

$1,000,000 Pension

Without
Wealth Creation

With
Wealth Creation

To Estate Taxes
$350,000

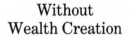

To Income Taxes
$350,000

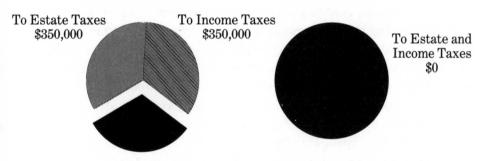

To Estate and
Income Taxes
$0

To Your Family

$300,000   vs $5,000,000

Prepared for: Client
Female Age 58

Based on Current Assumptions
© Barry Kaye Associates

REDUCE YOUR ESTATE TAX COST 80%, INCREASE YOUR NET ESTATE 280%

The following example shows a means of turning life insurance into an investment or further offsetting the estate taxes that ultimately will grow from the appreciation of one's estate.

In this situation, a man's estate is currently worth $10 million and his estate tax cost is approximately $5 million, leaving his children a net estate of $5 million (see chart, page 115).

Assuming the man is 60 years old and the return upon his and his wife's death would be approximately 10 to 1, based on current assumptions, he only requires $500,000 transferred to an Irrevocable Trust to purchase a life insurance policy of $5 million to pay the estate taxes at his death (proposal 1).

But he can also think in terms of additional insurance as an investment that is guaranteed, since death is guaranteed. Assuming that his gross estate will still be worth $10 million at his death, the resulting estate tax cost remains $5 million. However, he can buy $10 million of insurance in his estate tax free Irrevocable Trust at a cost of only $1 million (proposal 2).

The result at death is that his family receives after estate taxes $5 million plus $10 million in insurance proceeds estate tax free in his Trust. They receive a total of $15 million less the $1 million insurance cost for a net of $14 million, tax free.

In this manner, we have reduced his estate tax cost from $5 million to $1 million — 80% — and we have increased his net estate from $5 million to $14 million — a 280% increase!

Estate Taxation vs Wealth Creation

Reduce Your Estate Tax Cost 80%
Increase Your Net Estate 280%

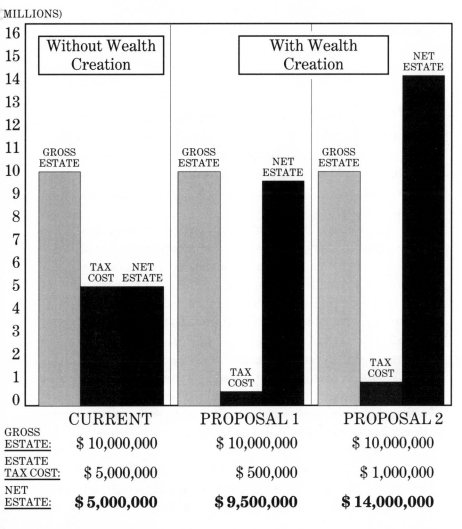

(MILLIONS)

	CURRENT	PROPOSAL 1	PROPOSAL 2
GROSS ESTATE:	$ 10,000,000	$ 10,000,000	$ 10,000,000
ESTATE TAX COST:	$ 5,000,000	$ 500,000	$ 1,000,000
NET ESTATE:	**$ 5,000,000**	**$ 9,500,000**	**$ 14,000,000**

Prepared for: Mr. & Mrs. Clients

Equal Age 60/60

Based on Current Assumptions
© 1990 Barry Kaye Associates

14

Who Is — and
Who Isn't — an Expert

When it comes to estate planning, most people consult with experts from various fields as to how best to proceed. Lawyers, accountants, investment brokers, insurance agents, and financial planners all are asked for their opinions and suggestions. Certainly, each area of expertise has its own impact on the overall program.

However, it is important to realize that most specialists are not experts in every field. While your attorney is probably very knowledgeable about the law, he or she may not be as conversant in matters of estate taxation and the key role life insurance can play in preserving wealth. This applies to investment brokers, accountants, and financial consultants who also may be stepping outside their field of expertise when they advise on matters of life insurance and its uses in discounting estate taxes.

There are many attorneys and accountants who specialize in estate planning. They are knowledgeable and should be used rather than generalists who have not had the experience to handle the practical, psychological, legal and humanistic aspects of this complicated field.

Just as the medical field is divided into areas of specialty, so, too, is the financial field. And just as you would consult the proper specialist for a medical problem, you should recognize the strengths and limitations of your financial advisors and seek professional assistance for each specific aspect of your financial situation.

This need to carefully screen your advisors also applies to some insurance salespeople and brokers. Not all of them are completely skilled in their understanding of this very specialized field, which includes a knowledge of the legal, technical, and tax ramifications of your estate planning decisions. It is crucial that your broker represent many companies so he can accomplish the diversification that has become so essential to this particular field. He must be knowledgeable about the different companies and their reinsurance carriers so that the underwriting can be achieved in the most expedient fashion. While price is important, in this case it is necessary to have a mix of the proper companies so that all of the medical and financial problems that can exist in consummating this amount of coverage are accommodated. Incorrect handling could forestall the program now or obstruct any future implementation of it. In addition, by representing only a single insurance company many agents are virtually unable to offer you the best policy for your situation or to follow a program of better protection through diversification.

There is one last point that needs to be made here. Often, when it comes to purchasing life insurance to discount estate taxes, extremely large sums of money are needed. Because of insurance carrier limits and cost averaging, the specifics of the purchase can be quite complex and will require extensive product knowledge, packaging finesse, volume power, and the ability to deal effectively with sophisticated and often conflicting reinsurance criteria in the proper order.

15

The Experts Agree

The articles on the following pages are written by eminent lawyers, an accountant, and a financial consultant knowledgeable in the field of estate taxation and familiar with the benefits of using life insurance to discount estate tax costs.

They provide some basic parameters of good estate planning as well as definitions of the various techniques of Generation Skipping, Grantor Retained Income Trusts, Charitable Remainder Trusts and Irrevocable Trusts. The articles include examples of cases these experts have been involved in and their solutions to various individuals' estate tax problems.

Perhaps you may find a situation described by these experts that is similar to your own, and you may be able to extrapolate essential information from it that will help you understand how this program can benefit you.

After reading this material, you will see that to an overwhelming degree these well-informed experts — from virtually every field of financial and estate planning — agree that this program is not only one of the most dramatic ways to create and preserve wealth, it is the only way. There really is no alternative.

AN OVERVIEW OF ESTATE
AND TAX PLANNING

BY BARRY H. BROWN, J.D.

Barry H. Brown, Attorney at Law, is a member of the State Bar of California and the Los Angeles County Bar Association. Mr. Brown is a principal with the law offices of Barry H. Brown, located in Century City, California. His practice emphasizes estate and tax planning for both individuals and businesses.

Most of you have worked hard your entire lifetime and have achieved a certain degree of financial security. The increase in your wealth has been a constant battle — tax strategy versus income tax induced erosion. You have accumulated an estate, but if it is not properly planned, much of your prior efforts may be rendered meaningless. By not correctly planning your affairs, you are subjecting your estate to unnecessary estate and inheritance taxes as well as probate costs.

The objective in estate planning is simple: to transfer one's assets at death, at the least expense and in the most efficient and effective manner, to the selected beneficiary, such as your spouse, child, or grandchild. However, as with everything in life, accomplishing the objective is not quite so simple.

There are a number of hurdles that must be overcome.

First, you must come to grips with the fact that someday you are going to die. Given that fact, the question is, Who am I going to leave my assets to? For most of us, the answer is easy: to our spouse or children. However, some of us may have to deal with extenuating circumstances regarding our next of kin. Perhaps our spouse and/or children are spendthrifts, drug addicts, or alcoholics, are suffering from some medical malaise, or belong to a cult. In any event, the first hurdle is to make a decision; almost any decision is better than none at all.

Second, you should be aware of the cost and expense of probating an estate. The primary costs of probating an estate are the fees and commissions of attorneys and executors or administrators. These fees, depending upon the particular jurisdiction, can range from 1% to 5% of the gross estate. Consider, for example, a $1.2 million estate in California. The statutory attorney's fees and executor's/administrator's commission are each computed as follows:

$$
\begin{array}{llll}
\text{First} & \$\ 15,000 \text{ at } 4\% & = & \$\ \ \ \ 600 \\
\text{Next} & \$\ 85,000 \text{ at } 3\% & = & \$\ 2,550 \\
\text{Next} & \$900,000 \text{ at } 2\% & = & \$18,000 \\
\text{Next} & \$200,000 \text{ at } 1\% & = & \underline{\$\ 2,000} \\
& \text{TOTAL} & & \$23,150
\end{array}
$$

Third, you must be aware of the effect of estate and inheritance taxes on your assets, that is, the toll the government extracts when property is transferred from one person to another at death.

Every person has an exemption that may either be used during one's lifetime against lifetime gifts, or can be offset against estate taxes at death. The current exemption equivalent is $600,000 (Unified Credit Amount of $192,800).

The Unified Credit Amounts are not set in concrete and therefore Congress can and, in all likelihood, will change them in the future. For example, under current law, the benefit of the Unified Credit Amount of $192,800 (exemption equivalent of $600,000) has been phased out for taxable estates in excess of $10 million but which do not exceed $21,040,000 ($18,340,000 after 1992). This is accomplished by raising the tax bracket to 60% on those amounts.

In one's overall estate plan, consideration should also be given to making gifts. One may make an annual gift of $10,000 to any number of persons. For example, a single person with two children could make gifts of $20,000 per year — $10,000 per child per year free of gift tax. A married couple with two children, on the other hand, can make gifts of $40,000 per year — $20,000 per child per year, free of gift tax. Gifts in excess of the annual per donee exclusion of $10,000 will be subject to gift tax; however, the lifetime exemption referred to above can be used to offset any potential gift tax. For example, if a single person gave a gift of $25,000 to his child in any one year, the amount in excess of the annual $10,000 permitted exclusion — $15,000 — would be subject to gift tax; however, no gift tax need be paid since the $15,000 can be offset against the $600,000 lifetime exemption amount.

Prior to relatively recent tax legislation, if one made a gift within three years of the date of death, there was a presumption that it was made "in contemplation of death" and therefore could be included back in one's estate. As a result of recent tax legislation, with one major exception, transfers made within three years of date of death are no longer included in one's taxable estate. However, there is an exception: life insurance. Thus, if existing life insurance is transferred within three years of the date of death, it will be included back in the decedent's gross estate for estate tax purposes.

In addition to the $600,000 exemption equivalent there is currently an Unlimited Marital Deduction between spouses, except when the surviving spouse is not a U.S. citizen. Therefore, now a married person may die and leave his or her entire estate, no matter how large, to his or her spouse and there will be no estate tax on the first death. This Unlimited Marital Deduction is very beneficial and can postpone estate taxes until the death of the second spouse. It is at the death of the second spouse that the day of reckoning will come. If no planning is done between husband and wife, there will be only one $600,000 exemption available; however, with proper planning and by establishing a Trust, we can utilize both the husband's and wife's exemptions and avoid estate taxes on estates of up to $1.2 million. By creating a Credit Shelter Trust or Bypass Trust, one can quickly and easily save substantial estate tax. By way of illustration only, on a $1.2 million estate one can save at least $255,000, as follows:

	First Death	Second Death
Without a Credit Shelter Trust:	no estate taxes	$255,000
With a Credit Shelter Trust:	no estate taxes	no estate taxes
Estate tax savings with a Credit Shelter Trust:		$255,000

If the surviving spouse is a non–U.S. citizen, the Unlimited Marital Deduction discussed above is lost. The loss of the deduction is effective for deaths occurring after November 10, 1988. In order to achieve deferral of the estate tax until the demise of the non–U.S. citizen surviving spouse, it will be necessary to establish a Qualified Domestic Trust (QDT).

In addition to the credit shelter or bypass Trust discussed above, married couples, especially if it is a second marriage or one spouse has significant separate property, may consider establishing a Qualified Terminal Interest Trust (QTIP Trust). In general, by creating a QTIP Trust the first spouse to die would, instead of leaving his or her property outright to the surviving spouse, be providing a lifetime income benefit for the surviving spouse. The primary advantage of the QTIP Trust is that it assures the decedent that on the death of the surviving spouse the remaining Trust property will be distributed to the decedent's designated beneficiaries, such as his or her children from a prior marriage as opposed to the children or new spouse of the surviving spouse.

An effective and relatively simple vehicle to accomplish most of the matters discussed above is the Revocable Living Trust. By creating a Revocable Living Trust and transferring one's property to the Trust, one can: (1) totally avoid probate; (2) minimize and in many cases completely avoid estate taxes; (3) obtain, in many cases, significant income tax benefits; (4) maintain complete privacy of one's affairs; and (5) avoid the requirement of a conservatorship.

Other effective tools in estate planning are life insurance

and the Irrevocable Life Insurance Trust. The Revocable Living Trust is a tremendous vehicle in estate planning; however, it has its limitations. For example, while a Revocable Living Trust can avoid probate on any size estate, it can only save estate taxes on estates of up to certain amounts: $600,000 for a single person and $1.2 million for a married couple. Thus, in general, estates in excess of those minimal threshold amounts will be subject to estate taxes even with the Revocable Living Trust.

A good estate planning technique is to utilize both the Revocable Living Trust and the Irrevocable Life Insurance Trust. By utilizing the Irrevocable Life Insurance Trust, you can keep life insurance benefits completely out of your estate. Thus the insurance policy death benefits can totally avoid income taxes as well as estate taxes. When creating the Irrevocable Life Insurance Trust, care should be taken to include a "Crummey Power" in the Trust so that the gift will qualify as a "present interest in property" and thus enable the donor to take advantage of his or her annual $10,000 per donee gift tax exclusion.

Another important estate planning tool that should be considered, especially in large estates, is the Charitable Remainder Trust. The Charitable Remainder Trust is a very flexible planning tool and when properly implemented will provide the donor with significant benefits, such as: (1) income tax savings, including capital gain avoidance; (2) estate tax savings; (3) additional cash flow; (4) retirement planning; (5) asset replacement; and (6) inflation hedge. The Charitable Remainder Trust is particularly appropriate if a person has appreciated assets. In this situation, the Charitable Remainder Trust and, in particular, the Unitrust, would work as follows: A donor would irrevocably transfer appreciated assets and pay no income tax. The donor, and possibly the donor's spouse, would receive an income each year determined by multiplying a fixed percentage, for example 8%, by the fair market value of the Trust assets valued annually. Upon the demise of the donor, the Trust assets would pass to the designated charity or charities free of estate taxes. In many instances, the donor would use the income tax savings resulting from the gift to charity to fund the premium for a life insurance policy that would replace the assets that ultimately pass to charity.

One additional technique worth mentioning is the Grantor-Retained Income Trust (GRIT). This type of Trust is used to reduce the combined transfer tax cost of transferring wealth through the current gift of a remainder interest in Trust. Briefly, a GRIT is an Irrevocable Trust whereby the grantor retains, for a term of years, the right to income. At the end of the term of years, the Trust would terminate and, typically, the Trust corpus would be distributable as a gift to a child or other beneficiary. If the grantor survives the term of years selected when the Trust was established, the Trust property, to include all appreciation during the term of years the property was in the Trust, would avoid estate tax on the demise of the grantor. Generally, the value of the gift is significantly less than the full value of the property transferred to the Trust. However, if the grantor does not survive the term of years selected, then the entire value of the property is included back in the grantor's estate for estate tax purposes.

A final note about the generation-skipping transfer-tax: In order to prevent a perceived abuse of the tax laws, Congress imposed a generation-skipping transfer tax on certain transfers, for example, transfers to grandchildren. However, each transferor has a $1 million generation-skipping transfer tax exemption. Therefore, a husband and wife together have $2 million of generation-skipping transfer tax exemptions. Proper planning will include provisions to preserve these exemptions, which otherwise may be lost.

Estate planning is a lifetime project. If properly designed and implemented, one cannot only avoid the hassles and costs of probate, but reduce and in many cases completely eliminate estate and inheritance taxes, thus transferring more wealth to loved ones.

TAX PLANNING FOR HARRY WEST: USING THE TAX LAWS FOR FAMILY AND CHARITY

BY MARVIN GOODSON, L.L.B.

Marvin Goodson is a principal in the tax law firm of Goodson and Wachtel in Los Angeles and is a widely recognized expert in tax and estate planning.

In the following illustration, the name of the donor and his company have been changed. The other facts and numbers are all accurate. These financial arrangements were developed between December 1, 1988 and May 1, 1989.

Harry West was the founding shareholder of West Widget Company. On December 1, 1988, Harry owned 80% of the stock in West Widget; 20% of the stock was owned by SC Holdings Inc., an unrelated corporation. Harry is married. He has four children, an ex-wife, a current wife, one sister, one brother, and 14 nieces, nephews, and cousins to whom he feels very close.

In October 1988, Harry had commenced initial negotiations for the sale of West Widget for a possible total of $85 million. The deal called for $20 million down, $35 million on a subordinated note with interest at 13%, and $30 million contingent earnout, payable over five years. Harry West is the key employee, president, chairman of the board, and CEO of West Widget.

Harry had not used any of his lifetime $600,000 gift and estate tax exemption, and neither had his wife. Harry had not made gifts in 1988 to any of his children, sister, brother, nephews, nieces, or cousins.

Two key requirements for any tax planning maneuvers were that Harry pay little or no current gift tax and that future death tax burdens be reduced significantly.

Initial planning problem: What recommendations could be made for Harry West?

An appraisal of his company was obtained immediately and

included valuing gifts of minority amounts of stock in the company. On a nonmarketable minority basis for gifts of around 8% of the stock of West Widget, a qualified independent nationally recognized appraisal firm appraised this 8% at $2 million. This was based on a nonmarketable, minority discounted value of the company of $25 million.

Phase I: Family Planning

Irrevocable Trusts with power to buy life insurance were formed for the benefit of Harry's four children. Harry contributed $1.2 million of stock at the $25 million value for the company (marketability, minority discount). The $1.2 million gift to the Trust did not result in a present gift tax since this utilized Harry's $600,000 lifetime exemption and his wife's $600,000 lifetime exemption by having her consent to the gift. (These exemptions will be recaptured on Harry's and his wife's deaths because of the sizes of their estates. However, any insurance proceeds will remain untaxed.)

The Children's Trusts were also exempt from the generation-skipping transfer tax, which means that the Trust, including growth and life insurance proceeds, can go on through many generations without further gift tax, death tax, or generation-skipping transfer tax imposed on it.

Layered on top of the Children's Trusts were four Special Trusts for the children. Stock transfers into the Special Trusts were $20,000 for each child (total $80,000) in December and $20,000 for each child ($80,000) in January. A total of $1,360,000 was transferred for the benefit of the four children through the use of Children's Trusts ($1.2 million) and Special Trusts ($160,000). Matters were simplified by setting forth both the Children's Trusts and the Special Trusts in one Combined Children's Trust document.

Harry named his attorney and accountant as the cotrustees and elected to have the income of the Combined Children's Trust accumulated and added to the principal. All distributions to the beneficiaries will be discretionary as determined by these independent trustees. The stated tests for distribution in the Trust require that the beneficiaries prove themselves to be good citizens and good family members, that they contribute personal services to society, and that they make the best of their abilities within their own lives. We call this the "good citizen" test. Under this test, financial success itself is not a necessary requirement.

Simultaneously with the forming of the Combined Children's Trust in December, 16 Irrevocable Relatives' Trusts were set up — all in one document — with the beneficiaries being Harry's sister, brother, and 14 nieces, nephews, and cousins. Harry transferred $20,000 in West Widget stock for each of the 16 beneficiaries in the Relatives' Trusts in December and in January. Accordingly, the total transferred to the Relatives' Trusts was $640,000, composed of $320,000 (16 × $20,000) in December and $320,000 in January. The same trust techniques used to establish the Children's Trusts were employed when structuring the Relatives' Trusts, so that no gift tax was payable.

As a result of the transfers to the Combined Children's Trust and Relatives' Trusts, $2 million in then value (8% of the company) was transferred to these 20 Trusts. This $2 million will bring $6.8 million of sale proceeds to the Trusts, subject to the same income tax on the gain as if Harry had sold the stock himself.

Income earned thereafter on the funds will either be kept in the Trusts or distributed to the beneficiaries depending upon the trustees' discretion. In this regard, other than the good citizen approach, the trustees will look to Harry for guidance as to when and how to make the distributions to the beneficiaries. The death tax savings on transferring these assets to the Trusts will be a minimum of $3,190,000. If, however, the Trusts invest their funds and the asset value doubles in 10 years, the death tax savings for Harry and his wife will be more than $7 million. If life insurance is purchased the savings will be multiplied many times over. In addition to these death tax savings, there are psychological benefits to Harry and his wife that are not measurable.

Phase II: Planning for Wealth Creation

The trustees plan on using $50,000 a year for 10 years to buy survivorship life insurance in the Children's Trusts on the lives of Harry and his wife. Barry Kaye is arranging for this $50,000 a year for 10 years to purchase over $20 million of life insurance, which will escape income taxes, death taxes, and generation-skipping transfer taxes. Although held in Trust for the children, the life insurance proceeds will be available to buy estate assets to provide funds for the payment of death taxes.

Phase III: Charitable Gifts

We suggested that Harry could benefit from the appreciated value of his stock by a one-time charitable contribution of some of his stock. This became Phase III.

Phase III of the planning required taking the opposite position to bring the stock up to its maximum value. The object was to set up a private charitable foundation so that Harry could transfer West Widget stock to the foundation at the maximum value; get a charitable-contribution deduction at the maximum value; have the foundation sell the stock in the sale without income tax or capital-gains tax; invest the sale proceeds; have the income from the investment available for distribution by Harry to public charities on an annual basis for the rest of his life and his wife's life; and on the death of Harry and his wife have the principal distributed to public charities. All the public charities were to be of Harry's and his wife's selection in each year.

Problems to be solved:

1. If Harry gave stock in his corporation to charity before a sale was agreed to, there would be the same marketable-minority discounts that applied to the gifts of company stock to the Trusts for family members. This means that Harry would get a much smaller charitable deduction for income tax purposes than the amount of money received by the charity.

2. If Harry gave $2 million (date-of-gift value) in stock to the foundation and the foundation received $6.8 million on the sale after the earnout and payouts, then the charitable foundation

would benefit, but Harry would only get a $2 million charitable contribution deduction.

3. If Harry gave stock to the charitable foundation after the sale was agreed to, then Harry would be taxed on the sale and all tax benefits from contributing appreciated property would be wiped out.

We overcame these problems as follows:

1. We recapitalized West Widget into two classes of stock: Class A common and Class B common. Class A common was entitled on sale or liquidation to all of the fixed or determinable amounts received on sale or liquidation (this would be the cash and notes). Class B common stock was entitled to all of the contingent amounts that were dependent on future events when the value could not be fixed and determinable at the date of the liquidation or sale. This was the earnout portion of the proposed sale.

2. The sales contract was negotiated completely down to the last point. However, the contract was not signed by anyone and there was no oral or written agreement of any kind that obligated either the buyer or the sellers. The officers of the new Harry West Foundation stated it was their "policy" to sell stock of this kind as the donor desired, although they were not "bound" to do so.

3. The buyer then issued a formal tender offer to all of the Class A and Class B shareholders of the company offering to buy the Class A stock for the total of $20 million down and $35 million in promissory notes, and the Class B stock for the $30 million earnout. The offer was contingent upon acceptance by all of the shareholders of the agreement that had been negotiated, but not signed.

4. Harry and the trustees of the 20 Trusts set up by Harry signed the tender offer accepting to sell stock and signed the sales agreement. The Trusts accepted for all of their Class A and Class B stock; Harry accepted for all of his Class B stock and roughly 96% of his Class A stock. Harry then made a contribution to the Harry West Foundation of approximately 4% of the

Class A stock retained by Harry, and he accompanied that contribution of Class A stock with the buyer's tender offer.

5. Within a couple of days, the Foundation accepted the tender offer and signed the sales agreement.

6. The value of the stock contributed to the charity at the tender offer price was appraised by the independent appraiser at $2 million. A charitable gift of $2 million gave Harry the full state and federal income tax deduction benefit of the $2 million contribution without having any alternative minimum tax.

From his 80% of the stock Harry gave 10% to the family members and 4% to charity, so he had 66% left. Harry's taxable income from the sale in the year of the sale will be in excess of $13 million from his 66% of the $20 million cash down payment. He will report the balance of the gain in the note receivable and the earnout when the cash is received in each year using the installment method of reporting.

Through the use of life insurance in the Children's Trusts, Harry's family will be protected from the usual death tax devastation...and all without financial strain on Harry.

Had Harry kept the $2 million of charitable contribution stock, he would have received $800,000 more cash on the sale (plus promissory notes) and would have owed $280,000 more combined state and federal (net effective) income tax in the year of sale, leaving him with $520,000 in cash from this one portion of the transaction. However, with the $2 million charitable contribution deduction, Harry's combined state and federal income taxes in the year of the sale will be diminished by $700,000. This means that, in the year of the sale, as a result of the contribution Harry has $180,000 more net cash in hand from the sale. The Harry West Foundation has $800,000 in cash and a promissory note for $1.2 million with interest at 13%. Assuming that the Foundation earns an average of 10% on the total of $2 million, there will be $200,000 annually that Harry will direct to public charities each year for the rest of his life, and his wife for the rest of her life. In addition, on their deaths (or earlier if they so desire), $2 million of principal will be distributed to public charities.

Appreciated stock in a closely held company can no longer be given to a typical private foundation the way it used to be. However, under a special section of the Internal Revenue Code, a private foundation under the umbrella of a public charity — such as Cedars Sinai Medical Center, The City of Hope, Vista Del Mar, California Institute of Technology, or a church or college — can receive stock in a closely held company and the donor will get the full charitable contribution deduction. In this instance, we used a well-known public charity that agreed that it would provide the special umbrella private foundation called the Harry West Foundation. The agreement with public charity provided that 10% of all income and principal distributions from the Harry West Foundation must go to this umbrella public charity. Harry West may direct more than 10% to this umbrella public charity in any year, but may direct no less than 10% of the income distributed and no less than 10% of the principal distributed.

Phase I, Phase II, or Phase III can be done independently of each other. It is not necessary that all be done. However, in the case of the Harry West family, this path was chosen because Harry wanted to get the benefit of all parts of the equation: (1) the low value for gifts to his family members, (2) the high value for contributions to his own private Foundation under the umbrella of a public charity, and (3) the possibility of substantial life insurance proceeds to escape income taxes, death taxes, and generation-skipping transfer taxes.

There are many variations of this example that are possible. Each step must be done carefully and with due regard to following precisely all of the tax cases, the tax code, and all of the rulings of the Internal Revenue Service so that there is relative certainty as to the end result. Even though the tax results are dramatic, the planning must be done conservatively. A similar structure can be used for an outright gift to a public charity. It is not necessary to use the special private foundation. The life insurance benefits can be achieved in several different ways.

For Phase I, Phase II, and Phase III maneuvers, it is important that there be no firm contract for the sale. Therefore, the earlier the problems can be attacked, more flexibility and increased benefits are assured to the stockholder.

DISCOUNTING YOUR ESTATE TAXES

BY JAMES Q. FISHER, ESQ.

James Q. Fisher, Esq., concentrates in aspects of tax planning. He is a principal with Levinson, Miller, Jacobs & Phillips, a law firm based in Century City, California.

In a recent actual case, Barry Kaye made a wealth creation proposal for a husband and wife. Mr. Kaye recommended the purchase of a Survivorship life insurance policy for the purpose of providing significant death benefits to be used by their family to pay a substantial portion of the anticipated estate costs associated with their estate.

Mr. Kaye discussed with them the extremely expensive nature of probate and estate costs, including estate taxes, state death taxes, legal, accounting and administration costs. For instance, such costs will deprive this family of fully 60% of the property for which they worked long and hard during their lives. Fortunately, one aspect of the current estate tax law, the Marital Deduction, provides some relief from these estate expenses. This deduction allows them to avoid estate taxes on any assets left to the surviving spouse. This effectively defers the estate tax liability until the passing of the second spouse.

An added benefit under the current federal estate tax structure allows each individual to leave up to $600,000 of estate assets to any beneficiary, either during life or upon death, without any estate tax cost whatsoever. However, Congress has considered proposals that would reduce or eliminate the $600,000 lifetime exclusion.

Based on these circumstances and the significant reduction

of the estate upon their deaths, it would be important to begin
now to provide for the future payments of these taxes and costs.
There are, of course, various ways this can be done. For instance,
they can begin investing today in a fund that, over time, will grow
to an amount that can be called upon by their family to pay some
or all of these final costs.

As an example, using Mr. Kaye's numbers, they could deposit
$264,225 in various savings vehicles such as CDs, treasury bills,
or government, corporate, or municipal bonds and, assuming an
after-tax yield of 8%, this fund would grow to approximately $5.2
million at the end of their joint life expectancies 40 years in the
future.

Mr. Kaye suggested an alternative: investing this same
amount of money in a life insurance policy that will pay as much as
$7 million upon the second of the two of them to pass away, regard-
less of whether they both pass away tomorrow or 40 years from
now. They can significantly enhance the power of these invested
dollars to pay estate taxes by placing this "investment fund,"
whether represented by an insurance policy or other savings type
investment, in an appropriately drawn Irrevocable Trust
designed to avoid estate taxes upon the fund. Without such an
estate tax savings trust, this fund would be taxed at more than
60%, leaving only approximately $2 million or $3 million relating
to the investment fund or the life insurance policy, respectively.
This money would be available to their family *after taxes* to pay
any ultimate estate tax liability on their remaining assets.

Mr. Kaye suggests that the acquisition of this life insurance
policy, which would pay as much as $7 million upon the second
death, is comparable to earning a $21 million profit. This is simply
another way of saying that the $7 million within an appropriately
drawn estate tax savings trust would pay the taxes on approximately $14 million of estate value (assuming a 50% estate tax
rate), which is the amount that would be left after earning a $21
million profit and paying one third of that, or $7 million, in capital
gains taxes.

Overall, it is true that a separate estate tax savings Irrevocable Trust could be created to which the clients could make gifts of cash that the trustee could at his discretion invest in a Survivorship life insurance policy. Further, such a properly drawn Trust would avoid estate taxes with respect to assets owned by it upon their death. As indicated above, this fund could grow to a substantial amount that could be used by their family to pay estate costs, including taxes. It is also true that a policy such as the one envisioned would pay its proceeds to the Trust without any income tax costs under Section 101 of the Internal Revenue Code, or any estate taxes. Consequently, the Trust assets would be fully available to their family to pay estate and probate costs and taxes.

It is indeed appropriate to consider various strategies to minimize estate tax costs and to provide the best possible means of taking care of their family and the estate costs associated with their passing. Mr. Kaye suggests, an investment fund properly structured to avoid estate taxes is a meritorious vehicle for doing so. The life insurance policy envisioned in this proposal appears to provide a very attractive accumulation vehicle for these purposes. Furthermore, Mr. Kaye has recommended that for an additional premium investment of approximately $55,000 they could insure the wife's life alone with the effect that, if she passes away first, the trust would have the immediate use of the policy proceeds of approximately $7 million, which could be further invested to fund estate taxes upon the later death of her husband.

It is important that they satisfy themselves that the insurance policy is an appropriate one for their needs and that they fully understand the guarantees, costs, and accumulation features associated with this policy. For the purpose of this discussion, I am assuming that this policy meets the proper tax definition of a life insurance policy under Section 7702 of the Internal Revenue Code. They should also consider the fact that in all probability prepayment of the policy premiums in the first few years of the policy could deprive them, or their Trust, of the ability to access the cash surrender value of the policy via loans, etc., without significant income tax consequences. On the other hand, prepayment of these premiums over five to seven years or more may not create a problem since these payments are based upon projected returns that have been estimated by Mr. Kaye to be higher than guaranteed returns.

PROTECTING YOUR ESTATE
BY DAVID DREMAN, INVESTMENT ADVISOR

David Dreman is managing director of Dreman Value Management, I.P. in New York. This article is reprinted with permission from Forbes *magazine.*

"Three generations from shirtsleeves to shirtsleeves." So the old saying goes. Grandpa made the family fortune, sonny squandered it and grandson is back on the assembly line. Is this tale apocryphal or true? The answer is, Sometimes true, most often not. The list of the rich does change rapidly over the decades, and very few of the superrich of one generation make the list several generations later, but you don't have to be in the Forbes 400 to pass on a reasonable nest egg to your heirs. What you do need is solid investment, legal, and financial planning.

Here are a few tips that have helped many of my clients.

A good way to start is to give systematic gifts to your children. The higher your income or net worth, the larger these gifts should be. You and your spouse are allowed to give a one-time gift of $600,000 each or a total of $1.2 million tax free to your beneficiaries, as well as $10,000 per year from each spouse to each child — indefinitely. If you have children, taking the maximum gift for a 20-year period, and compounding the money at 12%, they will have over $1.3 million. Not a bad start to a large fortune.

Sure, few of us have the luxury of giving $1.2 million and $20,000 a year to our young kin. But smaller one-time gifts and annual gifts thereafter add up to a sizeable nest egg, thanks to the magic of compound interest. A $200,000 gift and $10,000 a year, for example, become almost $3 million after 20 years (again compounded at 12%). Not a half-bad start for anyone.

A good safeguard for passing on capital to your heirs is a recently developed form of insurance (Joint Survivorship) combined with an Irrevocable Trust. You will need a good estate lawyer to handle the details. The concept is simple: If something happened to both you and your spouse, taxes would eat up a large part of your estate. But if you set up an Irrevocable Trust and assign the Survivorship insurance for both husband and wife to the Trust, it receives the insurance tax free, thus being able to pay all or part of the estate taxes. The Trust, however, must pay the premiums.

This insurance is relatively cheap for a couple in their 30s or 40s. If, for example, you are both 45 and take out $1 million of insurance for the Trust, you will pay premiums of about $4,600 a year for 9 to 10 years, after which the policy is paid in full. When the last spouse dies, the money goes to the Trust. Be sure to check payment schedules and rates with a number of insurance companies, as they can vary widely.

FOR TAX SAVINGS, CHARITY CAN BEGIN AT HOME
BY JOEL S. ISAACSON, C.P.A.

Joel S. Isaacson, C.P.A., is director of Personal Financial Planning for Weber, Lipshie & Co., a Certified Public Accounting firm with offices in New York and Beverly Hills, California.

Mitch and Sara Miller (age 68 and 67, respectively) currently have an estate worth approximately $9 million. Their wills have been set up to utilize both unified credits. They have moved to Florida to reduce their state estate tax expense and have been making annual gifts to their children and grandchildren. In addition, a 10-year Grantor Retained Income Trust was recently recommended by us for a valuable piece of real estate that they intended to hold. The property generates significant income each year.

At the same time they contemplated selling a piece of commercial real estate worth approximately $1 million. Their basis at the time was a negligible amount due to depreciation over many years. The couple also expressed a desire to advance certain charitable intentions as well as provide for their children and grandchildren.

We recommended both a Charitable Remainder Trust as well as a Generation Skipping Trust. In order to replace assets donated to the Charitable Trust, we recommended Survivorship life insurance owned by an Irrevocable Life Insurance Trust. An illustration of the advantages of the Charitable Remainder Annuity Trust follows.

CHARITABLE REMAINDER TRUSTS

A Charitable Remainder Trust is a Trust in which the grantor reserves for himself or the life of someone else the right to receive income for a period of time, perhaps for life, with the remainder ultimately going to charity. You receive a charitable contribution deduction (either an income tax or estate tax deduction) which is equal to the excess of the value (actuarily determined) of the property over the value of the retained right to receive the income. In order to receive the deduction for the value of the remainder interest given to charity, the Trust must be one of the following types of Charitable Remainder Trusts:

1) A Charitable Remainder Annuity Trust
2) A Charitable Remainder Unitrust
3) A Pooled Income Fund

Charitable Remainder Annuity Trust

A Charitable Remainder Annuity Trust is a Trust from which a fixed sum of not less than 5% of the net fair market value of the Trust, as valued when first placed in trust, is distributed annually to the noncharitable beneficiary, usually yourself or your spouse, with the remainder interest in the Trust ultimately going to a qualified charity. The annuitant receives a specified amount each year without regard to the actual income of the Trust.

Charitable Remainder Unitrust

A Charitable Remainder Unitrust is a Trust where a fixed percentage of not less than 5% of the fair market value of its assets valued each year is distributed to the noncharitable beneficiary, with the remainder interest ultimately going to a qualified charity.

The Unitrust concept permits the income beneficiary to receive a specified percentage of the total value of all assets in trust including accumulated income and unrealized appreciation or depreciation, which is determined as of a specified date each year without regard to the actual income of the Trust for the year. In this manner, the Unitrust, unlike the Annuity Trust, may function as a hedge against inflation.

Pooled Income Fund

A deduction is also allowed for the value of the remainder interest in property transferred to a Pooled Income Fund. A Pooled Income Fund is like a mutual fund run by a charitable organization which consists of gifts from many donors. You, or someone designated by you, receive all the income for a period of time, usually for life. When the income interest terminates, the charity receives the remainder interest attributable to that gift. A Pooled Income Fund gives you the advantages of a charitable remainder gift deduction without the administrative costs involved with setting up your own Charitable Trust.

The Pooled Interest Fund must be maintained by the public charity to which the irrevocable remainder interest is contributed. Each year, every income beneficiary receives an amount of income determined by the rate of return earned by the fund for that year.

PRINCIPAL ADVANTAGES OF CHARITABLE REMAINDER TRUSTS

Both the Charitable Remainder Annuity Trust and the Unitrust offer substantial tax and practical benefits. The Unitrust appears to have a distinct advantage in that income beneficiaries will receive higher benefits if Trust assets increase in value either because of good investment performance or further input of assets by the settler.

The practical and tax advantages of these Trusts can be summarized as follows:

1. Income tax deduction. Both offer significant income tax deductions, although each is computed somewhat differently.
2. Investment cash. The income tax deduction produces tax savings, which may be invested to produce additional income for the Trust beneficiaries or help fund the premiums for a Survivorship life insurance policy.
3. Avoidance of capital gains. Appreciated property may be transferred to the Trust without tax liability on the gain, subject, of course, to the percentage limitations and possibly the alternative minimum tax.
4. Diversification. The Trust may sell the assets transferred to it so as to provide greater diversification and, possibly, greater safety and higher income. This diversification is free of tax, which would not be the case if the settlor-donor had changed his portfolio.
5. Estate tax deduction. The settlor's estate is entitled to an estate tax deduction if the Trust assets are includible in the gross estate.

When one takes into account the income tax deduction and other advantages of the Trusts listed above, in some circumstance, their use may result in the settlor and his family actually receiving more money than the amount given to charity.

The results in any family situation depend on many factors, including the nature of the property transferred to the Trust, the size of the estate, and how long the income beneficiaries live.

NOTE: For valuations after May 1, 1989, the present value of the annuity is computed with new IRS tables that are based on a floating rate (120% of the federal mid-term rate). The attached illustrations are based on prior tables and used for illustration purposes only.

Asset Liquidation
vs
Charitable Remainder Annuity Trust (CRAT)

	CRAT	ASSET LIQUIDATION
Liquidation Value	$ 1,000,000	$ 1,000,000
Income Taxes Due	0	280,000
Investable Assets	1,000,000	720,000
Tax Deduction	244,000	0
Tax Savings	63,000	0
Investment Earnings	(a) 74,000	50,000
Life Insurance Cost	22,000	0
Net Cash Flow	52,000	50,000
10 Year Comparison		
Accumulation	718,000	1,416,000
Net After Estate Tax	323,00	637,000
Life Insurance	1,000,000	0
Net to Family	1,323,000	637,000

DIFFERENCE

$ 686,000

20 Year Comparison		
Accumulation	(b) 2,434,000	2,785,000
Net After Estate Tax	1,095,000	1,253,000
Life Insurance	1,000,000	0
Net to Family	2,095,000	1,253,000

DIFFERENCE

$ 842,000

Assumptions
1) Appreciated security (or real estate) with $1,000,000 value and no cost basis
2) Income tax bracket - 28%
3) After tax rate of return - 7%
4) All earnings are reinvested for comparison purposes
5) Estate tax bracket - 55%
6) Cost of $1,000,000 Last-To-Die policy - $22,000 payable for 10 years
7) Charitable deduction based on charitable remainder annuity trust, 10% Tables, 2 lives, Male age 68 and Female age 67
8) Contribution does not trigger the Alternative Minimum Tax

Notes
a) Investment earnings (under CRAT) include earnings on the tax savings
b) Net cash flow (under CRAT) in second 10 years does not include insurance cost, assume premium has vanished.

16

Give the Gift of Financial Security

One of the more phenomenal uses of life insurance in estate planning lies in the incredible leverage it offers as a means of optimizing the allowable tax exempt gifts you can make each year.

We've already discussed the fact that you can gift as many people as you desire with $10,000 a year under current law without having to pay any gift tax. Assuming that your chosen recipients — usually your children — need the money to maintain their lifestyle, gifting them outright is best. But if your children do not need the $10,000 at this time, the wealth-creation techniques discussed throughout this book can vastly increase the amount of the gift they ultimately receive.

The charts included on the following pages will show you exactly what kind of increase you can expect depending upon your specific situation. As an example, let's look at the way this program could be implemented by a husband and wife.

At an average 60 years of age, this couple statistically has a life expectancy of 20 more years. During the course of those 20 years they could gift $10,000 apiece to each of their children — $20,000 combined — gift tax free for a total of $400,000 for each child. While this is not an insubstantial amount of money, there are few families who would not choose to turn it into over $2 million if a method existed for doing so. One does.

Taking the $10,000 tax exempt yearly gift and purchasing life insurance provides a means of creating far greater wealth for the children upon the death of their parents.

Insurance purchased on the man using the $10,000 yearly amount over the projected 20-year period would result in proceeds to the children of $582,855. The same policy purchased on the woman, who is five years younger, would provide $1,112,490. This represents an increase of more than half a million dollars. Better still, if the insurance is purchased on both parents, the return will be $1,592,478, which will come to the children income and estate tax free. And this can be increased even more.

Remember, each parent can gift up to $10,000 per person per year. So if the man were to gift the $20,000 combined yearly from both he and his wife and his children were to purchase the same insurance policy, they, upon his death, would receive $1,165,710 estate tax free. If the insurance were purchased on his wife's life, the children would receive $2,224,980. But if this couple were to purchase a Last-To-Die policy insuring both their lives, the insurance proceeds on their $400,000 total, 20-year investment would be a guaranteed return of $3,184,956.

As an additional bonus, the man has decreased his estate by $400,000, gift tax free. This means that the $200,000 of estate taxes that his children would have had to pay on the money if it had been left in his estate are avoided completely. In effect, the $3,184,956 of insurance proceeds is purchased with only the $200,000 that would have remained after estate taxes.

Where else can you invest $20,000 a year and have your children receive over $3 million on a guaranteed basis based on current assumptions? Nowhere, and that's just another example of the incredible power of life insurance.

O.M.E - Optimium Money Engineering
Income-Gift-Estate Tax Free
Through December 31

$10,000 Annual Contribution
Produces Death Benfits of...

AGE	MALE	FEMALE	LAST-TO-DIE
10	$ 10,550,000	$ 11,710,000	
20	6,798,000	8,322,000	
30	3,928,000	5,622,000	
40	2,021,000	2,990,000	$ 3,482,972
50	1,061,230	1,538,720	2,094,241
55	788,245	1,112,470	1,592,978
60	582,855	818,056	1,082,772
65	431,326	603,496	727,466
70	314,011	441,852	479,545
75	228,059	321,032	320,596
80	165,695	229,089	

*The Amazing Leverage of Life Insurance
and Tax Free Gifts!**

* If completed annually by December 31
Under the Uniform Gift Tax Law
All figures are based on current assumptions

O.M.E - Optimium Money Engineering
Income-Gift-Estate Tax Free
Through December 31

$20,000 Annual Contribution
Produces Death Benfits of...

AGE	MALE	FEMALE	LAST-TO-DIE
10	$ 21,100,000	$ 23,420,000	
20	3,399,000	4,161,000	
30	1,964,000	2,811,000	
40	1,010,000	1,495,000	$ 6,965,944
50	2,122,460	3,077,440	4,188,482
55	1,576,490	2,224,940	3,185,956
60	1,165,710	1,636,110	2,165,544
65	862,652	1,206,990	1,454,932
70	628,022	883,704	959,190
75	456,118	642,064	641,191
80	331,390	458,179	

*The Amazing Leverage of Life Insurance
and Tax Free Gifts!**

* If completed annually by December 31
Under the Uniform Gift Tax Law
All figures are based on current assumptions

17

Immortality — Gift
$1 Million to Charity
at a Cost of $65,000

There is yet another means of using the program described here to optimize financial and estate planning when charitable giving is a concern. Let's look at a means by which the leverage of life insurance can dramatically increase your ability to make contributions to your favorite charitable institutions without it costing you anything more.

One client wanted to make a contribution to his local hospital. He had committed $100,000 to them, which could be paid in one year or over a five-year period. Upon further consideration, he decided to purchase for that same $100,000 a $1 million life insurance policy and make a contribution that is much more meaningful. The contribution was earmarked for an endowment fund and the monies were not needed immediately, so there was no reason why the funds could not come to the institution at a later date upon his death. More important, the client was delighted with the opportunity to make a substantially greater contribution than would otherwise have been possible.

He purchased a Last-To-Die policy for himself and his wife with a return of approximately 10 to 1. This produced $1 million for a cost of $100,000, which could be paid at the rate of $20,000 a year for six years or discounted, on a One Pay basis, to the $100,000, based on current assumptions. In his tax bracket, the net cost of the $100,000 contribution to purchase the policy was effectively only $65,000 because he would have lost almost a full third of the $100,000 to income taxes had he not donated it in this manner.

It is obvious how you can optimize your gifts to charity by purchasing insurance on your life, your spouse's life, or both lives.

These policies also produce substantial cash values that generally exceed the actual premiums after the fourth or fifth year. This means that there is cash value equity against which the institutions can borrow in case they need emergency money.

One of our clients was a university professor who was very inclined toward giving large amounts of money to his university. Through this method, he was able to achieve a substantial discount that would be provided by utilizing a life insurance policy to purchase a much greater amount of money that would go to the institution after his death. In this way, he could greatly increase the potential end result for his beloved school.

He arranged his programs at a much lower outlay by paying the premiums over a lifetime.

18

Good for You,
Good for America

From the time of "taxation without representation" through TEHRA '89, our most recent Federal tax code "reforms," thoughtful Americans have attempted to find a balance between the financial needs of their nation and their own personal desire to minimize their tax burden.

There are those who would see the tax exempt nature of certain aspects of life insurance benefits ended in an attempt to increase the coffers of the U.S. government. They claim that this tax exempt status serves only to preserve the fortunes of the wealthy at the expense of the rest of the country. If they succeed in their efforts to make the proceeds from life insurance taxable, it will hurt America immeasurably.

Insurance proceeds have always been income tax free. They augment Social Security benefits. They provide a method for private enterprise to subsidize the financial problems of many widows and orphans who have lost their providers prematurely, leaving them with no form of income for their basic sustenance. Life insurance is purchased with after-tax dollars and therefore is receiving nothing more than the stepped-up basis of any financial product available at one's death.

What would the government really accomplish if it attacked the Irrevocable Trust and other methods of eliminating insurance from one's estate?

Uncle Sam would realize immediate extra revenue from the estate tax levied on the insurance proceeds. However, by reducing the amount of the inherited estate, the government loses for all time the additional income taxes it would realize on the fully intact estate.

For example, if the government were to tax a $5 million life insurance benefit at the current rate of 50%, it would realize a $2.5 million tax increase. However, that same $5 million left in the estate will, over a period of 20 years, alone earn approximately $10 million of interest income (based on a 10% investment return of $500,000 per year). The income tax paid on this amount would be $3.3 million — $800,000 more than the amount the government would receive by taxing the life insurance benefits.

Over a 40-year period of earning our assumed 10% interest, the $5 million insurance proceeds will earn $20 million of interest income. The tax would be at least $6.6 million — fully $4.1 million in increased tax revenues.

Yet, even as dynamic as it is, the above example pales in comparison to the numerous additional benefits the U.S. economy realizes when the untaxed life insurance proceeds are available for reinvestment in capital growth.

With the increased interest income on the untaxed life insurance proceeds, dramatically heightened levels of capital exist to invest in business and financial opportunities. This in turn helps create both profits and jobs, thereby broadening the entire tax base for the country. Additional dollars are realized on the corporate income tax generated as a result of such investment as well as on the income taxes paid by an expanded work force.

As an example, suppose your heirs inherited the $5 million (estate tax free) of life insurance discussed earlier and invested the $500,000 interest income it generated in a manufacturing business with annual sales of $5 million. At a 15% profit margin, this company would have taxable income of $750,000, the tax on which is approximately $210,000. In addition, let's assume that this company would have a modest ratio of employee to sales, and

would employ 15 people. The president of the firm would earn
$100,000 annually. The vice president of sales and the chief
financial officer each would earn $50,000 a year. Two department
heads each would make $35,000 a year and the remaining staff of
10 would average $30,000 annual income. Their combined
$570,000 annual earnings would result in approximately $450,000
of adjusted gross income, generating approximately $126,000 in
federal income taxes.

This company would pay $336,000 per year in total combined
corporate and individual income taxes. Without any adjustments
for potential growth, this means a total of $4.2 million over a
20-year period.

And this example only illustrates the use of one year's worth
of interest income generated by the $5 million. During the same
20-year period, that income amount would increase to $10 million.
Imagine the increased taxes that amount would generate as it was
similarly invested.

But this is only the start, for we are not simply talking about
the investment potential of one estate. As the untaxed life insurance proceeds from estates all across the nation are effectively
pooled, the tax revenues generated increase even more
dramatically.

Now think of how this applies when utilizing larger estates of
$50 million to $100 million and more. A $100 million estate pays
taxes of approximately $55 million. Once the government has col-
lected that $55 million, they will experience no further benefits
from the money. The tax proceeds will be spent as a part of the
budget for the current year, never to be utilized again. Using our
approach, the tax advantages available with this method still provide the same tax revenue for the government. However, through
the private enterprise of the insurance industry, the taxes that
the government has received will be replaced by the insurance
company for the individual's estate. This money can now work in
perpetuity to produce all the advantages of investment in
America and the resulting taxes created from those investments.

But these are not the only benefits that are realized by leaving life insurance proceeds outside the grasp of estate taxation through techniques such as the Irrevocable Trust.

Life insurance proceeds are paid to the beneficiary in cash. For most estates, the bulk of the assets are not held in cash but rather in property or investments. Without the cash to pay the estate taxes, the illiquid estate may have to sell assets at distressed prices. This in turn devalues the estate and lessens the amount of estate taxes the government realizes.

Furthermore, the illiquid estate may have to defer or delay the payment of its taxes. During this time, the government loses the full use of the money.

If, however, the life insurance and Trust proceeds are not taxed, they can be used to immediately pay the estate taxes in full. What the government appears to lose in taxes on the insurance benefits it more than makes up in maintaining the true value of the estate and receiving its tax payments promptly and at their optimum levels.

These incentives certainly add to the attractiveness of purchasing insurance by the American public. Clearly, leaving the tax free status of life insurance benefits unmolested is not only good for you, it is good for America.

Unfettered by immediate taxation, the wealth created and preserved by using life insurance as a tool to discount estate taxes will produce far greater revenues, a healthier economy, and a broader job and tax base for every segment of our population than would otherwise be the case. Even the most inflated estimates of immediate revenues from the taxation of these proceeds cannot equal the immense long-term gains to be realized. In the final analysis, this far-reaching vision will generate greater dollars to power America's future.

19

Compare and Save

There are approximately 2,000 life insurance companies in America. I have utilized for our examples most of the leading companies. They include Alexander Hamilton, Confederation Life, Connecticut Mutual, Crown Life, Equitable, First Colony, General America, Guardian, Jackson National, Manufacturers Life, Metropolitan Life, Mutual of New York, Mutual Benefit, New England Life, North American Life, Occidental-Transamerica, Phoenix Mutual, Prudential, State Mutual, and Sun Life, and many more.

The rates listed on the ensuing pages are based upon their proposals circa January 1, 1990. Obviously, these rates, the dividends, and the interest factors, as well as the mortality rates, can change. Some of these policies may not be available in your state. Also, since these rates can be so different at the time you are reading this, I have chosen not to name the companies. These figures therefore should be used only as examples, not as final determining figures. In order to be positive of the current rates, you should check them at the time you read this book or become interested in implementing a plan. I have tried to ascertain the lowest premiums for comparative purposes. Obviously, the higher the premium, in most cases, the larger the cash value. Lower premiums usually produce a lower cash value.

There are many variables besides price that must be taken into consideration. These rates are based on nonsmoker and preferred health situations. Any variation from that profile could change the rates substantially and make one company more desirable than the next. Furthermore, all rates are based on current assumptions; different companies having different experiences over a period of time can produce different results than their original projections. In most instances, as I have discussed earlier, I recommend that you diversify your insurance portfolio by utilizing three to five insurance companies that produce the best melded rates. In this manner, you are spreading the risk as well as assuring yourself of a better potential result over a period of years.

Once again, these rates are based on current assumptions of mortality and interest. Any changes in these assumptions could result in higher premiums, longer payment periods, or lower death benefits. Remember, while there are stringent rules that apply to the insurance companies' portfolio behavior, and certain reserves that must be met in accordance with each state's regulations, the guarantees from an insurance company are based on their own financial statements and backed only by the assets and financial strength of that company. Once again, this is why we recommend that you look for the strongest companies rated by Best, Standard and Poor's, and Moody's, and further realize that the lowest price may not be in your best long-term interest. Obviously, utilizing three or four companies should help rectify this risk and give you the most conservative and prudent approach to purchasing your life insurance.

With this in mind, you will now find the different rates for Male, Female, and Last-To-Die policies based on $1 million. They are shown in five-year increments on a One Pay, Limited Pay and 25-Payment/Lifetime Pay basis. You should be able to extrapolate at any age for any type of policy with any type of payment method that you prefer in order to estimate the approximate cost of implementing this program for yourself, your family, or your client.

A.M. Best

Rating of Insurance Companies

INSURANCE COMPANY	RATING
Acacia Mutual Life	A+
Aetna Life	A+
Alexander Hamilton	A+
Allstate Life	A+
American General Life	A+
Bankers Life & Casualty	A+
Beneficial Standard	A+
Berkshire Life	A+
Canada Life Assurance	A+
Central Life Assurance	A+
Columbus Mutual	A+
Combined Insurance	A+
Confederation Life	A+
Connecticut General Life	A+
Connecticut Mutual Life	A+
Crown Life	A+
Equitable Life Assurance	A+
Equitable Life of Iowa	A+
Equitable of Colorado	A+
Fidelity & Guaranty	A+
First Colony	A+
General American Life	A+
Guardian Life	A+
Hartford Life	A+
Home Life	A+
Indianapolis Life	A+
Jackson National	A+
John Hancock Life	A+
Kansas Life	A+
Life Insurance Co. of Virginia	A+

Rating of Insurance Companies (*Cont.*)

INSURANCE COMPANY	RATING
Lincoln Benefit	A+
Lincoln National	A+
Lincoln Security of New York	A+
Lincoln Security of Connecticut	A+
Manufacturers Life	A+
Mass Mutual Life	A+
Metropolitan Life	A+
Midland Mutual	A+
Minnesota Mutual Life	A+
Mutual Benefit Life	A+
Mutual Life of New York	A+
National Life	A+
New England Mutual	A+
New York Life	A+
North American Co. Life & Health	A+
Northwestern Mutual	A+
Pacific Mutual Life	A+
Pan American Life	A+
Penn Mutual Life	A+
Phoenix Mutual Life	A+
Principal Mutual	A+
Provident Mutual	A+
Prudential Insurance	A+
Safeco Life Insurance	A+
Security Connecticut Life	A+
Security Life of Denver	A+
Southland Life	A+
State Farm Life	A+
State Mutual Life	A+
Sun Life Assurance	A+
Transamerica Occidental	A+
Travelers Insurance	A+
US Life	A+

Source: A.M. Best Company - by permission

Standard & Poor's Corporation

Life Insurance Company Claims
Paying Ability Rating

Aetna Life Insurance Company	AAA
American Life Insurance Company	AAA
Commonwealth Life Insurance Company	AAA
Confederation Life Insurance & Annuity Company	AAA
Connecticut General Life Insurance Company	AAA
Confederation Life Insurance Company	AAA
Continental Assurance Company (Interco Pool)	AAA
Crown Life Insurance Company (Canada)	AAA
Dai-Ichi Life Insurance Company (Japan)	AAA
Great-West Life Assurance Company (Canada)	AAA
Hartford Life Insurance Company	AAA
John Hancock Mutual Life Insurance Company	AAA
Lincoln Benefit Life Insurance Company	AAA
Lincoln National Pension Insurance Company	AAA
Manufacturers Life Insurance Company	AAA
Massachusetts Mutual Life Insurance Company	AAA
Metropolitan Life Insurance Company	AAA
Minnesota Mutual Life Insurance Company	AAA
Mutual of America Life Insurance Company	AAA
Mutual Benefit Life	AAA
Mutual Life of New York	AAA
New York Life Insurance Company	AAA
Northwestern Mutual Life Insurance Company	AAA
Pacific Mutual Life	AAA

Life Insurance Company Claims
Paying Ability Rating (*Cont.*)

INSURANCE COMPANY	CPA RATING
Peoples Security Life Insurance Company	AAA
Phoenix Mutual Life Insurance Company	AAA
Principal Mutual Life Insurance Company	AAA
Provident Life and Accident	AAA
Provident National Assurance	AAA
Prudential Insurance Company of America	AAA
Security Life of Denver	AAA
State Mutual Life Assurance	AAA
Sumitomo Life Assurance Company (Japan)	AAA
Sun Life Assurance Company of Canada	AAA
Yasuda Mutual Life Insurance Company, Limited	AAA
Connecticut Mutual Life Insurance Company	AA+
Lincoln National Life Insurance	AA+
Mutual Life Company of New York	AA+
New England Mutual Life Insurance Company	AA+
Blue Cross of Western Pennsylvania	AA
Sun Life Insurance Company of America	A+
Massachusetts Indemnity & Life Insurance Company	A+

Source: Standard & Poor's Corporation - by permission

Life Insurance Financial Strength Ratings

COMPANY	FINANCIAL RATING
Aetna Life Insurance Company	Aaa
Allstate Life Insurance Company	Aaa
Associated Insurance Companies, Inc.	Aa3
Commonwealth Life Insurance Company	Aa3
Connecticut General Life Insurance Company	Aaa
Connecticut Mutual Life Insurance Company	Aa2
Continental Assurance Company	Aa1
Equitable Life Assurance Society of the U.S.	Aa3
General American Life Insurance Company	Aa3
Guardian Life Insurance Company of America	Aaa
Hartford Life Insurance Company	Aa2
Home Life Insurance Company	Aa3
John Hancock Mutual Life Insurance Company	Aaa
Life Insurance Company of Virginia	Aa3
Lincoln National Life Insurance Company	Aa3
Massachusetts Mutual Life Insurance Company	Aaa
Metropolitan Life Insurance Company	Aaa
Minnesota Mutual Life Insurance Company	Aa1
Mutual Benefit Life Insurance Company	Aa2
Mutual Life Insurance Company of New York	Aa2
Nationwide Life Insurance Company	Aaa
New York Mutual Life Insurance Company	Aa1
New York Life Insurance Company	Aaa
Northwestern Mutual Life Insurance Company	Aaa

Life Insurance Financial Strength Ratings (*Cont.*)

COMPANY	FINANCIAL RATING
Ohio National Life Insurance Company	Aa2
Pacific Mutual Life Insurance Company	Aa2
Pan-American Life Insurance Company	A1
Penn Mutual Life Insurance Company	A1
Peoples Security Life Insurance Company	Aa3
Phoenix Mutual Life Insurance Company	Aa1
Principal Mutual Life Insurance Company	Aaa
Provident Life & Accident Insurance Company	Aa1
Provident National Assurance Company	Aa1
Prudential Insurance Company of America	Aaa
Southwestern Life Insurance Company	Baa3
State Mutual Life Assurance Company of America	Aa1
Sun Life Insurance Company of America	A1
Transamerica Life Insurance and Annuity Company	Aa3
Transamerica Occidental Life Insurance Company	Aa3
Travelers Insurance Company	Aa2
UNUM Life Insurance Company	Aa1
UNUM Life Insurance Company of America	Aaa
Western National Life Insurance Company	Baa1
Zurich American Life Insurance Company	Aa3

Source: Moody's Investors Service - by permission

$1,000,000 Death Benefit Costs
One Payment
Male Age 30

INSURANCE COMPANY	ANNUAL PREMIUM	NUMBER OF YEARS	TOTAL PAYMENTS
Company A	$ 26,738	1	$ 26,738
Company B	27,337	1	27,337
Company C	30,470	1	30,470
Company D	31,106	1	31,106
Company E	31,399	1	31,399
Company F	32,024	1	32,024
Company G	33,237	1	33,237
Company H	35,468	1	35,468
Company I	35,753	1	35,753
Company J	46,350	1	46,350
Company K	56,386	1	56,386
Company L	57,728	1	57,728
Company M	58,185	1	58,185
Company N	58,842	1	58,842
Company O	60,874	1	60,874
Company P	63,611	1	63,611
Company Q	66,307	1	66,307
Company R	67,038	1	67,038
Company S	74,262	1	74,262
Company T	74,920	1	74,920

All figures based on current assumptions

$1,000,000 Death Benefit Costs
One Payment
Male Age 40

INSURANCE COMPANY	ANNUAL PREMIUM	NUMBER OF YEARS	TOTAL PAYMENTS
Company A	$ 47,834	1	$ 47,834
Company B	48,437	1	48,437
Company C	54,837	1	54,837
Company D	55,753	1	55,753
Company E	58,650	1	58,650
Company F	59,686	1	59,686
Company G	59,828	1	59,828
Company H	64,956	1	64,956
Company I	65,065	1	65,065
Company J	78,580	1	78,580
Company K	88,176	1	88,176
Company L	90,054	1	90,054
Company M	93,675	1	93,675
Company N	93,995	1	93,995
Company O	99,422	1	99,422
Company P	103,123	1	103,123
Company Q	103,789	1	103,789
Company R	105,808	1	105,808
Company S	111,183	1	111,183
Company T	112,328	1	112,328

All figures based on current assumptions

$1,000,000 Death Benefit Costs
One Payment
Male Age 50

INSURANCE COMPANY	ANNUAL PREMIUM	NUMBER OF YEARS	TOTAL PAYMENTS
Company A	$ 91,360	1	$ 91,360
Company B	92,617	1	92,617
Company C	101,551	1	101,551
Company D	102,031	1	102,031
Company E	102,468	1	102,468
Company F	106,330	1	106,330
Company G	110,716	1	110,716
Company H	117,095	1	117,095
Company I	121,077	1	121,077
Company J	140,270	1	140,270
Company K	146,509	1	146,509
Company L	147,984	1	147,984
Company M	149,398	1	149,398
Company N	158,186	1	158,186
Company O	160,416	1	160,416
Company P	164,946	1	164,946
Company Q	170,137	1	170,137
Company R	172,557	1	172,557
Company S	181,819	1	181,819
Company T	185,031	1	185,031

All figures based on current assumptions

$1,000,000 Death Benefit Costs
One Payment
Male Age 55

INSURANCE COMPANY	ANNUAL PREMIUM	NUMBER OF YEARS	TOTAL PAYMENTS
Company A	$ 125,474	1	$ 125,474
Company B	129,634	1	129,634
Company C	133,089	1	133,089
Company D	139,169	1	139,169
Company E	139,679	1	139,679
Company F	139,857	1	139,857
Company G	149,834	1	149,833
Company H	153,260	1	153,260
Company I	159,947	1	159,947
Company J	189,619	1	189,619
Company K	191,127	1	191,127
Company L	192,528	1	192,528
Company M	196,910	1	196,910
Company N	201,518	1	201,518
Company O	208,974	1	208,974
Company P	208,979	1	208,979
Company Q	217,826	1	217,826
Company R	222,309	1	222,309
Company S	224,817	1	224,817
Company T	233,388	1	233,388

All figures based on current assumptions

$1,000,000 Death Benefit Costs
One Payment
Male Age 60

INSURANCE COMPANY	ANNUAL PREMIUM	NUMBER OF YEARS	TOTAL PAYMENTS
Company A	$ 170,024	1	$ 170,024
Company B	174,369	1	174,369
Company C	178,332	1	178,332
Company D	183,198	1	183,198
Company E	183,739	1	183,739
Company F	193,295	1	193,295
Company G	198,842	1	198,842
Company H	200,123	1	200,123
Company I	207,649	1	207,649
Company J	213,488	1	213,488
Company K	237,023	1	237,023
Company L	253,063	1	253,063
Company M	256,175	1	256,175
Company N	264,600	1	264,600
Company O	273,431	1	273,431
Company P	273,877	1	273,877
Company Q	275,880	1	275,880
Company R	291,002	1	291,002
Company S	305,855	1	305,855
Company T	314,391	1	314,391

All figures based on current assumptions

$1,000,000 Death Benefit Costs
One Payment
Male Age 65

INSURANCE COMPANY	ANNUAL PREMIUM	NUMBER OF YEARS	TOTAL PAYMENTS
Company A	$ 226,563	1	$ 226,563
Company B	240,300	1	240,300
Company C	240,691	1	240,691
Company D	241,089	1	241,089
Company E	255,205	1	255,205
Company F	256,144	1	256,144
Company G	260,847	1	260,847
Company H	262,495	1	262,495
Company I	263,646	1	263,646
Company J	273,431	1	273,431
Company K	298,396	1	298,396
Company L	335,080	1	335,080
Company M	349,481	1	349,481
Company N	363,084	1	363,084
Company O	375,513	1	375,513
Company P	375,900	1	375,900
Company Q	376,590	1	376,590
Company R	385,607	1	385,607
Company S	403,866	1	403,866
Company T	409,529	1	409,529

All figures based on current assumptions

$1,000,000 Death Benefit Costs
One Payment
Male Age 70

INSURANCE COMPANY	ANNUAL PREMIUM	NUMBER OF YEARS	TOTAL PAYMENTS
Company A	$ 294,875	1	$ 294,875
Company B	308,937	1	308,937
Company C	316,305	1	316,305
Company D	216,715	1	316,715
Company E	331,521	1	331,521
Company F	334,017	1	334,017
Company G	334,335	1	334,335
Company H	337,824	1	337,824
Company I	338,966	1	338,966
Company J	392,155	1	392,155
Company K	457,397	1	457,397
Company L	472,126	1	472,126
Company M	498,600	1	498,600
Company N	527,720	1	527,720
Company O	539,497	1	539,497
Company P	540,913	1	540,913
Company Q	543,606	1	543,606
Company R	625,460	1	625,460
Company S	635,545	1	635,545

All figures based on current assumptions

$1,000,000 Death Benefit Costs
One Payment
Male Age 75

INSURANCE COMPANY	ANNUAL PREMIUM	NUMBER OF YEARS	TOTAL PAYMENTS
Company A	$ 375,278	1	$ 375,278
Company B	385,615	1	385,615
Company C	404,105	1	404,105
Company D	405,385	1	405,385
Company E	414,934	1	414,934
Company F	441,553	1	441,553
Company G	448,159	1	448,159
Company H	451,865	1	451,865
Company I	543,162	1	543,162
Company J	596,386	1	596,386
Company K	699,026	1	699,026
Company L	700,044	1	700,044
Company M	750,268	1	750,268
Company N	777,699	1	777,699
Company O	952,480	1	952,480
Company P	984,025	1	984,025

All figures based on current assumptions

$1,000,000 Death Benefit Costs
One Payment
Male Age 80

INSURANCE COMPANY	ANNUAL PREMIUM	NUMBER OF YEARS	TOTAL PAYMENTS
Company A	$ 494,136	1	$ 494,136
Company B	511,378	1	511,378
Company C	516,120	1	516,120
Company D	551,549	1	551,549
Company E	568,357	1	568,357
Company F	865,699	1	865,699
Company G	992,780	1	992,780
Company H	1,015,685	1	1,015,685
Company I	1,594,652	1	1,594,652

Death benefits can increase as payments exceed $1,000,000
All figures based on current assumptions

$1,000,000 Death Benefit Costs
Limited Payments
Male Age 30

INSURANCE COMPANY	ANNUAL PREMIUM	NUMBER OF YEARS	TOTAL PAYMENTS
Company A	$ 4,471	8	$ 35,768
Company B	4,492	8	35,936
Company C	7,300	5	36,500
Company D	6,563	6	39,378
Company E	4,749	9	42,741
Company F	5,500	8	44,000
Company G	5,864	8	46,912
Company H	5,879	8	47,032
Company I	9,530	6	57,180
Company J	5,582	7	65,960
Company K	9,708	7	67,956
Company L	8,800	8	70,400
Company M	10,425	7	72,975
Company N	10,876	7	76,132
Company O	8,245	10	82,450
Company P	7,526	11	82,786
Company Q	11,850	7	82,950
Company R	8,593	10	85,930
Company S	7,951	11	87,461
Company T	10,816	9	97,344

All figures based on current assumptions

$1,000,000 Death Benefit Costs
Limited Payments
Male Age 40

INSURANCE COMPANY	ANNUAL PREMIUM	NUMBER OF YEARS	TOTAL PAYMENTS
Company A	$ 7,933	8	$ 63,464
Company B	8,168	8	65,344
Company C	10,077	7	70,539
Company D	12,160	6	72,960
Company E	12,253	6	73,253
Company F	8,455	9	76,095
Company G	9,844	8	78,752
Company H	10,691	8	85,528
Company I	10,775	8	86,200
Company J	14,580	6	87,480
Company K	13,683	8	109,464
Company L	16,117	7	112,819
Company M	14,208	8	113,664
Company N	17,048	7	119,336
Company O	15,835	8	126,680
Company P	16,660	8	133,280
Company Q	13,328	10	133,280
Company R	13,736	10	137,360
Company S	12,609	11	138,699
Company T	16,337	9	147,033

All figures based on current assumptions

$1,000,000 Death Benefit Costs
Limited Payments
Male Age 50

INSURANCE COMPANY	ANNUAL PREMIUM	NUMBER OF YEARS	TOTAL PAYMENTS
Company A	$ 15,028	8	$ 120,224
Company B	20,640	6	123,840
Company C	15,927	8	127,416
Company D	18,974	7	132,818
Company E	22,830	6	136,980
Company F	15,565	9	140,085
Company G	17,916	8	143,328
Company H	19,357	8	154,856
Company I	20,189	8	161,512
Company J	24,770	7	173,390
Company K	22,172	8	177,376
Company L	27,012	7	189,084
Company M	23,698	8	189,584
Company N	27,210	8	195,648
Company O	25,795	8	206,360
Company P	21,640	10	216,400
Company Q	24,360	9	219,240
Company R	25,913	9	233,217
Company S	23,517	10	235,170
Company T	21,440	12	257,280

All figures based on current assumptions

$1,000,000 Death Benefit Costs
Limited Payments
Male Age 55

INSURANCE COMPANY	ANNUAL PREMIUM	NUMBER OF YEARS	TOTAL PAYMENTS
Company A	$ 27,050	6	$ 162,300
Company B	20,742	8	165,936
Company C	22,446	8	179,568
Company D	25,961	7	181,727
Company E	31,031	6	186,186
Company F	23,630	8	189,040
Company G	21,477	9	193,293
Company H	25,449	8	195,592
Company I	26,742	8	213,936
Company J	28,573	8	228,584
Company K	32,910	7	230,370
Company L	34,162	7	239,134
Company M	30,688	8	245,504
Company N	31,409	8	251,272
Company O	29,720	9	267,480
Company P	27,209	10	272,090
Company Q	31,130	9	280,170
Company R	35,525	8	284,200
Company S	33,348	9	300,132
Company T	32,733	10	327,330

All figures based on current assumptions

$1,000,000 Death Benefit Costs
Limited Payments
Male Age 60

INSURANCE COMPANY	ANNUAL PREMIUM	NUMBER OF YEARS	TOTAL PAYMENTS
Company A	$ 35,440	6	$ 212,640
Company B	28,329	8	226,632
Company C	34,369	7	240,583
Company D	31,212	8	249,696
Company E	41,738	6	250,428
Company F	31,309	8	250,472
Company G	33,350	8	266,800
Company H	30,043	9	270,387
Company I	34,752	8	278,016
Company J	39,718	7	278,026
Company K	37,325	8	298,600
Company L	43,100	7	301,700
Company M	44,732	7	313,124
Company N	44,985	7	314,895
Company O	42,613	8	340,904
Company P	38,050	9	342,450
Company Q	43,469	8	347,752
Company R	38,280	10	382,800
Company S	37,213	11	409,343
Company T	49,781	10	497,810

All figures based on current assumptions

173

$1,000,000 Death Benefit Costs
Limited Payments
Male Age 65

INSURANCE COMPANY	ANNUAL PREMIUM	NUMBER OF YEARS	TOTAL PAYMENTS
Company A	$ 38,257	8	$ 306,056
Company B	46,008	7	322,056
Company C	46,180	7	323,260
Company D	41,501	8	332,008
Company E	55,433	6	332,598
Company F	42,901	8	343,208
Company G	44,370	8	354,960
Company H	44,501	8	356,008
Company I	52,028	7	364,196
Company J	40,614	9	365,526
Company K	49,885	8	399,080
Company L	61,444	7	430,108
Company M	57,666	8	461,328
Company N	57,900	8	463,200
Company O	58,877	8	471,016
Company P	59,915	8	479,320
Company Q	48,510	11	533,610
Company R	52,050	11	572,550
Company S	51,597	12	619,164
Company T	71,826	10	718,260

All figures based on current assumptions

$1,000,000 Death Benefit Costs
Limited Payments
Male Age 70

INSURANCE COMPANY	ANNUAL PREMIUM	NUMBER OF YEARS	TOTAL PAYMENTS
Company A	$ 50,814	8	$ 406,612
Company B	60,656	7	424,592
Company C	61,130	7	427,910
Company D	71,904	6	431,424
Company E	55,345	8	442,760
Company F	56,969	8	455,752
Company G	57,871	8	462,968
Company H	58,080	8	464,640
Company I	69,878	7	489,146
Company J	55,701	9	501,309
Company K	79,435	7	556,045
Company L	70,627	8	565,016
Company M	88,401	7	618,807
Company N	58,140	11	639,540
Company O	75,445	9	679,005
Company P	77,674	9	699,066
Company Q	80,460	10	804,600
Company R	67,050	12	804,600
Company S	113,441	10	1,134,410

Death benefits can increase as payments exceed $1,000,000
All figures based on current assumptions

$1,000,000 Death Benefit Costs
Limited Payments
Male Age 75

INSURANCE COMPANY	ANNUAL PREMIUM	NUMBER OF YEARS	TOTAL PAYMENTS
Company A	$ 66,625	8	$ 533,000
Company B	78,427	7	548,989
Company C	79,900	7	559,300
Company D	70,463	8	563,704
Company E	74,719	8	597,752
Company F	77,880	8	623,040
Company G	83,386	8	667,088
Company H	95,528	7	668,696
Company I	79,030	9	711,270
Company J	107,515	7	752,605
Company K	93,911	9	845,199
Company L	76,460	12	917,520
Company M	98,558	10	985,580
Company N	106,799	10	1,067,990
Company O	87,220	13	1,133,860
Company P	90,570	13	1,177,410
Company Q	113,480	11	1,248,280
Company R	169,657	10	1,696,570

Death benefits can increase as payments exceed $1,000,000
All figures based on current assumptions

$1,000,000 Death Benefit Costs
Limited Payments
Male Age 80

INSURANCE COMPANY	ANNUAL PREMIUM	NUMBER OF YEARS	TOTAL PAYMENTS
Company A	$ 104,900	6	$ 629,400
Company B	89,079	8	712,632
Company C	98,992	8	791,936
Company D	104,192	8	848,327
Company E	106,899	9	962,091
Company F	149,215	7	1,044,505
Company G	132,434	9	1,191,906
Company H	106,080	12	1,272,960
Company I	129,927	10	1,299,270
Company J	118,940	12	1,427,280
Company K	147,838	11	1,626,218
Company L	258,741	10	2,587,410

Death benefits can increase as payments exceed $1,000,000

All figures based on current assumptions

$1,000,000 Death Benefit Costs
25 Payments
Male Age 30

INSURANCE COMPANY	ANNUAL PREMIUM	NUMBER OF YEARS	TOTAL PAYMENTS
Company A	$ 2,229	25	$ 55,725
Company B	2,414	25	60,362
Company C	2,857	25	71,425
Company D	2,905	25	72,620
Company E	2,990	25	74,738
Company F	3,218	25	80,450
Company G	3,260	25	81,500
Company H	3,383	25	84,575
Company I	3,606	25	90,159
Company J	3,695	25	92,375
Company K	3,972	25	99,289
Company L	5,367	25	134,175
Company M	5,619	25	140,475
Company N	6,001	25	150,025

All figures based on current assumptions

$1,000,000 Death Benefit Costs
25 Payments
Male Age 40

INSURANCE COMPANY	ANNUAL PREMIUM	NUMBER OF YEARS	TOTAL PAYMENTS
Company A	$ 4,437	25	$ 110,916
Company B	4,441	25	111,025
Company C	5,112	25	127,800
Company D	5,225	25	130,625
Company E	5,488	25	137,204
Company F	5,991	25	149,775
Company G	5,994	25	149,850
Company H	6,245	25	156,125
Company I	6,458	25	161,450
Company J	6,645	25	166,125
Company K	7,151	25	178,775
Company L	8,458	25	211,450
Company M	8,740	25	218,500
Company N	9,337	25	233,425

All figures based on current assumptions

$1,000,000 Death Benefit Costs
25 Payments
Male Age 50

INSURANCE COMPANY	ANNUAL PREMIUM	NUMBER OF YEARS	TOTAL PAYMENTS
Company A	$ 8,530	25	$ 213,260
Company B	9,348	25	233,700
Company C	9,540	25	238,500
Company D	10,046	25	251,150
Company E	10,345	25	258,622
Company F	11,054	25	276,350
Company G	11,381	25	284,525
Company H	11,919	25	297,975
Company I	12,215	25	305,375
Company J	12,253	25	306,325
Company K	12,698	25	317,450
Company L	13,588	25	339,700
Company M	14,476	25	361,900
Company N	14,851	25	371,275

All figures based on current assumptions

$1,000,000 Death Benefit Costs
25 Payments
Male Age 55

INSURANCE COMPANY	ANNUAL PREMIUM	NUMBER OF YEARS	TOTAL PAYMENTS
Company A	$ 12,041	25	$ 301,025
Company B	13,365	25	334,125
Company C	13,554	25	338,850
Company D	13,867	25	346,680
Company E	13,942	25	348,550
Company F	15,793	25	394,825
Company G	14,770	25	369,250
Company H	16,092	25	402,300
Company I	16,715	25	417,875
Company J	17,021	25	425,525
Company K	17,105	25	427,625
Company L	17,653	25	441,325
Company M	19,027	25	475,675
Company N	19,897	25	497,425

All figures based on current assumptions

$1,000,000 Death Benefit Costs
25 Payments
Male Age 60

INSURANCE COMPANY	ANNUAL PREMIUM	NUMBER OF YEARS	TOTAL PAYMENTS
Company A	$ 16,836	25	$ 420,900
Company B	18,763	25	469,076
Company C	18,984	25	474,600
Company D	19,220	25	480,500
Company E	19,282	25	482,050
Company F	19,769	25	494,225
Company G	21,554	25	538,850
Company H	21,914	25	547,850
Company I	22,825	25	570,625
Company J	23,265	25	581,625
Company K	24,131	25	603,275
Company L	24,891	25	622,275
Company M	24,937	25	623,425
Company N	29,548	25	738,700

All figures based on current assumptions

$1,000,000 Death Benefit Costs
25 Payments
Male Age 65

INSURANCE COMPANY	ANNUAL PREMIUM	NUMBER OF YEARS	TOTAL PAYMENTS
Company A	$ 23,506	25	$ 587,650
Company B	25,485	25	637,430
Company C	26,382	25	659,550
Company D	26,900	25	672,500
Company E	27,312	25	682,800
Company F	28,549	25	713,725
Company G	28,632	25	715,800
Company H	30,774	25	769,350
Company I	31,158	25	778,950
Company J	31,169	25	779,225
Company K	32,445	25	811,125
Company L	33,127	25	828,175
Company M	34,281	25	857,025
Company N	41,816	25	1,045,400

Death benefits can increase as payments exceed $1,000,000
All figures based on current assumptions

$1,000,000 Death Benefit Costs
25 Payments
Male Age 70

INSURANCE COMPANY	ANNUAL PREMIUM	NUMBER OF YEARS	TOTAL PAYMENTS
Company A	$ 32,623	25	$ 815,575
Company B	35,452	25	886,306
Company C	36,348	25	908,700
Company D	37,182	25	929,550
Company E	38,672	25	966,800
Company F	38,707	25	967,675
Company G	40,730	25	1,018,250
Company H	41,095	25	1,027,375
Company I	41,820	25	1,045,500
Company J	44,966	25	1,124,150
Company K	45,073	25	1,126,825
Company L	45,615	25	1,140,375
Company M	49,356	25	1,233,900
Company N	64,400	25	1,610,000

Death benefits can increase as payments exceed $1,000,000
All figures based on current assumptions

$1,000,000 Death Benefit Costs
25 Payments
Male Age 75

INSURANCE COMPANY	ANNUAL PREMIUM	NUMBER OF YEARS	TOTAL PAYMENTS
Company A	$ 46,287	25	$ 1,157,175
Company B	50,528	25	1,263,193
Company C	50,547	25	1,263,675
Company D	51,673	25	1,291,825
Company E	53,520	25	1,338,000
Company F	58,648	25	1,466,200
Company G	59,100	25	1,477,500
Company H	59,688	25	1,492,200
Company I	63,865	25	1,596,625
Company J	66,214	25	1,655,350
Company K	70,495	25	1,762,375
Company L	72,323	25	1,808,075
Company M	94,479	25	2,361,975

Death benefits can increase as payments exceed $1,000,000

All figures based on current assumptions

185

$1,000,000 Death Benefit Costs
20 Payments
Male Age 80

INSURANCE COMPANY	ANNUAL PREMIUM	NUMBER OF YEARS	TOTAL PAYMENTS
Company A	$ 76,440	20	$ 1,528,800
Company B	78,298	20	1,565,954
Company C	79,424	20	1,588,487
Company D	86,588	20	1,731,760
Company E	119,610	20	2,392,200
Company F	159,072	20	3,181,440

Death benefits can increase as payments exceed $1,000,000

All figures based on current assumptions

$1,000,000 Death Benefit Costs
One Payment
Female Age 30

INSURANCE COMPANY	ANNUAL PREMIUM	NUMBER OF YEARS	TOTAL PAYMENTS
Company A	$ 20,758	1	$ 20,758
Company B	21,675	1	21,675
Company C	24,289	1	24,289
Company D	25,729	1	25,729
Company E	26,461	1	26,461
Company F	27,745	1	27,745
Company G	27,795	1	27,795
Company H	28,400	1	28,400
Company I	28,796	1	28,796
Company J	38,380	1	38,380
Company K	46,024	1	46,024
Company L	49,547	1	49,547
Company M	51,422	1	51,422
Company N	53,385	1	53,385
Company O	54,274	1	54,274
Company P	55,018	1	55,018
Company Q	56,094	1	56,094
Company R	56,297	1	56,297
Company S	60,940	1	60,940
Company T	62,174	1	62,174

All figures based on current assumptions

$1,000,000 Death Benefit Costs
One Payment
Female Age 40

INSURANCE COMPANY	ANNUAL PREMIUM	NUMBER OF YEARS	TOTAL PAYMENTS
Company A	$ 36,354	1	$ 36,354
Company B	36,682	1	36,682
Company C	42,490	1	42,490
Company D	43,250	1	43,250
Company E	44,252	1	44,252
Company F	48,247	1	48,247
Company G	48,652	1	48,652
Company H	49,594	1	49,594
Company I	51,268	1	51,268
Company J	66,870	1	66,870
Company K	71,603	1	71,603
Company L	73,330	1	73,330
Company M	75,198	1	75,198
Company N	77,975	1	77,975
Company O	80,202	1	80,202
Company P	83,359	1	83,359
Company Q	86,214	1	86,214
Company R	88,731	1	88,731
Company S	90,412	1	90,412
Company T	90,936	1	90,936

All figures based on current assumptions

$1,000,000 Death Benefit Costs
One Payment
Female Age 50

INSURANCE COMPANY	ANNUAL PREMIUM	NUMBER OF YEARS	TOTAL PAYMENTS
Company A	$ 67,270	1	$ 67,270
Company B	68,113	1	68,113
Company C	79,776	1	79,776
Company D	80,967	1	80,967
Company E	82,067	1	82,067
Company F	85,671	1	85,671
Company G	87,268	1	87,268
Company H	87,281	1	87,281
Company I	95,199	1	95,199
Company J	116,650	1	116,650
Company K	121,251	1	121,251
Company L	126,079	1	126,079
Company M	126,966	1	126,966
Company N	132,006	1	132,006
Company O	133,656	1	133,656
Company P	136,715	1	136,715
Company Q	137,604	1	137,604
Company R	140,041	1	140,041
Company S	140,505	1	140,505
Company T	141,626	1	141,626

All figures based on current assumptions

$1,000,000 Death Benefit Costs
One Payment
Female Age 55

INSURANCE COMPANY	ANNUAL PREMIUM	NUMBER OF YEARS	TOTAL PAYMENTS
Company A	$ 94,244	1	$ 94,244
Company B	95,025	1	95,025
Company C	106,760	1	106,760
Company D	107,468	1	107,468
Company E	107,258	1	107,258
Company F	114,623	1	114,623
Company G	114,755	1	114,755
Company H	116,153	1	116,153
Company I	126,843	1	126,843
Company J	159,214	1	159,214
Company K	160,594	1	160,594
Company L	160,640	1	160,640
Company M	161,429	1	161,429
Company N	161,820	1	161,820
Company O	167,476	1	167,476
Company P	169,201	1	169,201
Company Q	173,675	1	173,675
Company R	179,461	1	179,461
Company S	183,295	1	183,295
Company T	184,579	1	184,579

All figures based on current assumptions

$1,000,000 Death Benefit Costs
One Payment
Female Age 60

INSURANCE COMPANY	ANNUAL PREMIUM	NUMBER OF YEARS	TOTAL PAYMENTS
Company A	$ 132,266	1	$ 132,266
Company B	133,199	1	133,199
Company C	142,861	1	142,861
Company D	144,219	1	144,219
Company E	145,881	1	145,881
Company F	152,497	1	152,497
Company G	155,218	1	155,218
Company H	157,931	1	157,931
Company I	167,707	1	167,707
Company J	203,747	1	203,747
Company K	204,975	1	204,975
Company L	205,165	1	205,165
Company M	205,760	1	205,760
Company N	209,796	1	209,796
Company O	210,550	1	210,550
Company P	215,567	1	215,567
Company Q	220,050	1	220,050
Company R	228,189	1	228,189
Company S	230,048	1	230,048
Company T	239,220	1	239,220

All figures based on current assumptions

$1,000,000 Death Benefit Costs
One Payment
Female Age 65

INSURANCE COMPANY	ANNUAL PREMIUM	NUMBER OF YEARS	TOTAL PAYMENTS
Company A	$ 181,850	1	$ 181,850
Company B	186,541	1	186,541
Company C	192,198	1	192,198
Company D	192,937	1	192,937
Company E	196,804	1	196,804
Company F	208,452	1	208,452
Company G	208,977	1	208,977
Company H	215,552	1	215,552
Company I	220,297	1	220,297
Company J	253,862	1	253,862
Company K	264,927	1	264,927
Company L	270,417	1	270,417
Company M	275,900	1	275,900
Company N	283,856	1	283,856
Company O	293,063	1	293,063
Company P	293,526	1	293,526
Company Q	294,907	1	294,907
Company R	307,967	1	307,967
Company S	317,444	1	317,444
Company T	320,819	1	320,819

All figures based on current assumptions

$1,000,000 Death Benefit Costs
One Payment
Female Age 70

INSURANCE COMPANY	ANNUAL PREMIUM	NUMBER OF YEARS	TOTAL PAYMENTS
Company A	$ 243,738	1	$ 243,738
Company B	256,786	1	256,786
Company C	260,116	1	260,116
Company D	261,151	1	261,151
Company E	270,360	1	270,360
Company F	272,170	1	272,170
Company G	279,531	1	279,531
Company H	280,281	1	280,281
Company I	287,064	1	287,064
Company J	302,265	1	302,265
Company K	374,188	1	374,188
Company L	383,503	1	383,503
Company M	393,670	1	393,670
Company N	398,136	1	398,136
Company O	403,114	1	403,114
Company P	427,388	1	427,388
Company Q	427,825	1	427,825
Company R	437,065	1	437,065
Company S	440,960	1	440,960
Company T	496,849	1	496,849

All figures based on current assumptions

$1,000,000 Death Benefit Costs
One Payment
Female Age 75

INSURANCE COMPANY	ANNUAL PREMIUM	NUMBER OF YEARS	TOTAL PAYMENTS
Company A	$ 320,195	1	$ 320,195
Company B	334,645	1	334,645
Company C	350,877	1	350,877
Company D	351,024	1	351,024
Company E	353,038	1	353,038
Company F	371,961	1	371,961
Company G	389,075	1	389,075
Company H	389,886	1	389,886
Company I	431,841	1	431,841
Company J	538,979	1	538,979
Company K	574,425	1	574,425
Company L	582,314	1	582,314
Company M	593,321	1	593,321
Company N	638,872	1	638,872
Company O	667,890	1	667,440
Company P	690,440	1	690,440

All figures based on current assumptions

$1,000,000 Death Benefit Costs
One Payment
Female Age 80

INSURANCE COMPANY	ANNUAL PREMIUM	NUMBER OF YEARS	TOTAL PAYMENTS
Company A	$ 439,003	1	$ 439,003
Company B	439,805	1	439,805
Company C	490,525	1	490,525
Company D	497,424	1	497,424
Company E	514,402	1	514,402
Company F	703,778	1	703,778
Company G	800,893	1	800,893
Company H	818,317	1	818,317
Company I	906,423	1	906,423
Company J	1,157,036	1	1,157,036

Death benefits can increase as payments exceed $1,000,000

All figures based on current assumptions

$1,000,000 Death Benefit Costs
Limited Payments
Female Age 30

INSURANCE COMPANY	ANNUAL PREMIUMS	NUMBER OF YEARS	TOTAL PAYMENTS
Company A	$ 3,493	8	$ 27,944
Company B	3,543	8	28,344
Company C	6,210	5	31,050
Company D	4,439	7	31,073
Company E	5,602	6	33,612
Company F	4,253	8	34,024
Company G	4,559	8	36,472
Company H	4,698	8	37,584
Company I	4,357	9	39,213
Company J	7,580	6	45,480
Company K	7,736	7	54,152
Company L	8,588	7	60,116
Company M	8,737	7	61,159
Company N	6,635	10	66,350
Company O	9,523	7	66,661
Company P	6,455	11	71,005
Company Q	8,065	9	72,585
Company R	6,624	11	72,864
Company S	10,690	7	74,830
Company T	8,972	9	80,748

All figures based on current assumptions

$1,000,000 Death Benefit Costs
Limited Payments
Female Age 40

INSURANCE COMPANY	ANNUAL PREMIUM	NUMBER OF YEARS	TOTAL PAYMENTS
Company A	$ 6,003	8	$ 48,024
Company B	6,188	8	49,504
Company C	10,150	5	50,750
Company D	7,782	7	54,474
Company E	7,422	8	59,378
Company F	10,181	6	61,084
Company G	7,922	8	63,376
Company H	7,378	9	66,402
Company I	8,480	8	67,841
Company J	11,870	7	83,090
Company K	13,515	7	84,247
Company L	12,318	7	86,226
Company M	13,631	7	95,417
Company N	16,920	7	102,388
Company O	10,404	10	104,040
Company P	9,688	11	106,568
Company Q	13,625	8	109,000
Company R	10,470	11	109,447
Company S	14,560	8	116,480
Company T	13,241	9	119,169

All figures based on current assumptions

$1,000,000 Death Benefit Costs
Limited Payments
Female Age 50

INSURANCE COMPANY	ANNUAL PREMIUM	NUMBER OF YEARS	TOTAL PAYMENTS
Company A	$ 11,525	8	$ 92,200
Company B	11,169	8	89,352
Company C	16,680	6	100,080
Company D	14,691	7	102,837
Company E	17,977	6	107,860
Company F	13,612	8	108,896
Company G	14,381	8	115,048
Company H	13,043	9	117,387
Company I	15,788	8	126,304
Company J	19,650	7	137,550
Company K	21,235	7	144,655
Company L	21,651	7	151,557
Company M	20,368	8	162,944
Company N	24,960	7	166,126
Company O	20,875	8	167,000
Company P	16,878	10	168,780
Company Q	21,330	8	170,640
Company R	17,370	10	170,833
Company S	20,294	9	182,646
Company T	16,813	12	201,756

All figures based on current assumptions

$1,000,000 Death Benefit Costs
Limited Payments
Female Age 55

INSURANCE COMPANY	ANNUAL PREMIUM	NUMBER OF YEARS	TOTAL PAYMENTS
Company A	$ 15,624	8	$ 124,992
Company B	16,200	8	129,600
Company C	21,800	6	130,800
Company D	19,865	7	139,055
Company E	23,983	6	143,898
Company F	17,988	8	143,906
Company G	18,920	8	151,360
Company H	17,533	9	157,797
Company I	21,064	8	168,511
Company J	29,710	7	192,626
Company K	27,735	7	194,145
Company L	27,025	8	194,767
Company M	25,320	8	202,560
Company N	28,995	7	202,965
Company O	25,718	8	205,744
Company P	22,860	10	208,142
Company Q	22,601	10	226,010
Company R	25,594	9	230,346
Company S	25,990	9	233,910
Company T	26,890	9	242,010

All figures based on current assumptions

$1,000,000 Death Benefit Costs
Limited Payments
Female Age 60

INSURANCE COMPANY	ANNUAL PREMIUM	NUMBER OF YEARS	TOTAL PAYMENTS
Company A	$ 21,855	8	$ 174,840
Company B	29,650	6	177,900
Company C	23,033	8	184,264
Company D	26,811	7	187,677
Company E	32,151	6	192,907
Company F	24,189	8	193,515
Company G	25,276	8	202,208
Company H	24,328	9	218,952
Company I	27,852	8	222,813
Company J	38,280	7	244,032
Company K	36,066	7	252,462
Company L	34,855	8	254,370
Company M	32,178	8	257,424
Company N	32,546	8	262,080
Company O	32,864	8	262,912
Company P	38,705	7	270,935
Company Q	30,600	10	284,917
Company R	33,290	9	299,610
Company S	33,870	9	304,830
Company T	31,179	10	311,790

All figures based on current assumptions

$1,000,000 Death Benefit Costs
Limited Payments
Female Age 65

INSURANCE COMPANY	ANNUAL PREMIUM	NUMBER OF YEARS	TOTAL PAYMENTS
Company A	$ 40,000	6	$ 240,000
Company B	30,339	8	242,712
Company C	36,185	7	253,295
Company D	32,528	8	260,224
Company E	43,538	6	261,225
Company F	32,767	8	262,135
Company G	35,030	8	280,240
Company H	35,867	8	286,938
Company I	34,585	9	310,815
Company J	40,258	8	322,064
Company K	49,800	7	322,904
Company L	48,014	7	336,098
Company M	46,095	8	343,028
Company N	43,370	8	346,960
Company O	43,900	8	351,200
Company P	51,745	7	362,215
Company Q	42,580	9	383,220
Company R	44,730	9	402,570
Company S	41,910	10	404,118
Company T	45,815	10	458,150

All figures based on current assumptions

$1,000,000 Death Benefit Costs
Limited Payments
Female Age 70

INSURANCE COMPANY	ANNUAL PREMIUM	NUMBER OF YEARS	TOTAL PAYMENTS
Company A	$ 54,950	6	$ 329,700
Company B	41,254	8	330,032
Company C	48,917	7	342,419
Company D	57,652	6	345,910
Company E	44,796	8	358,365
Company F	52,608	7	368,256
Company G	46,528	8	372,224
Company H	46,769	8	374,150
Company I	47,800	8	382,400
Company J	46,057	9	414,513
Company K	64,521	7	451,647
Company L	64,850	8	465,312
Company M	58,583	8	468,664
Company N	61,845	8	486,288
Company O	53,040	10	530,400
Company P	60,960	9	548,640
Company Q	72,045	8	576,360
Company R	59,730	11	657,030
Company S	70,431	10	704,310
Company T	58,710	12	704,520

All figures based on current assumptions

$1,000,000 Death Benefit Costs
Limited Payments
Female Age 75

INSURANCE COMPANY	ANNUAL PREMIUM	NUMBER OF YEARS	TOTAL PAYMENTS
Company A	$ 55,264	8	$ 442,112
Company B	75,600	6	453,600
Company C	65,340	7	457,380
Company D	65,586	7	459,102
Company E	59,286	8	474,288
Company F	61,756	8	494,046
Company G	75,538	7	528,766
Company H	69,550	8	556,400
Company I	65,558	9	590,022
Company J	95,695	7	669,865
Company K	87,150	9	716,108
Company L	85,985	9	735,198
Company M	82,314	9	740,826
Company N	71,710	11	788,810
Company O	63,370	13	823,810
Company P	87,890	10	878,900
Company Q	80,970	12	971,640
Company R	112,224	10	1,122,240

Death benefits can increase as payments exceed $1,000,000

All figures based on current assumptions

$1,000,000 Death Benefit Costs
Limited Payments
Female Age 80

INSURANCE COMPANY	ANNUAL PREMIUM	NUMBER OF YEARS	TOTAL PAYMENTS
Company A	$ 75,802	8	$ 606,413
Company B	101,100	6	606,600
Company C	79,687	8	637,496
Company D	89,403	8	729,193
Company E	93,452	9	841,068
Company F	125,955	7	881,685
Company G	120,550	9	987,842
Company H	119,025	9	997,486
Company I	101,000	11	1,112,100
Company J	118,704	10	1,187,040
Company K	96,190	13	1,250,470
Company L	182,293	10	1,822,930

Death benefits can increase as payments exceed $1,000,000
All figures based on current assumptions

$1,000,000 Death Benefit Costs
25 Payments
Female Age 30

INSURANCE COMPANY	ANNUAL PREMIUM	NUMBER OF YEARS	TOTAL PAYMENTS
Company A	$ 1,751	25	$ 43,775
Company B	1,873	25	46,850
Company C	2,307	25	57,675
Company D	2,462	25	61,550
Company E	2,532	25	63,300
Company F	2,621	25	65,525
Company G	2,700	25	67,500
Company H	3,055	25	76,375
Company I	3,067	25	76,675
Company J	3,490	25	87,281
Company K	4,262	25	106,550
Company L	4,584	25	114,604
Company M	5,281	25	132,025
Company N	8,139	25	203,475

All figures based on current assumptions

$1,000,000 Death Benefit Costs
25 Payments
Female Age 40

INSURANCE COMPANY	ANNUAL PREMIUM	NUMBER OF YEARS	TOTAL PAYMENTS
Company A	$ 3,285	25	$ 82,125
Company B	3,313	25	82,825
Company C	4,142	25	103,550
Company D	4,419	25	110,475
Company E	4,734	25	118,350
Company F	4,899	25	122,475
Company G	5,338	25	133,450
Company H	5,475	25	136,875
Company I	4,456	25	111,400
Company J	6,333	25	158,325
Company K	6,583	25	164,575
Company L	6,741	25	168,525
Company M	8,119	25	202,975
Company N	8,916	25	222,900

All figures based on current assumptions

$1,000,000 Death Benefit Costs
25 Payments
Female Age 50

INSURANCE COMPANY	ANNUAL PREMIUM	NUMBER OF YEARS	TOTAL PAYMENTS
Company A	$ 6,102	25	$ 152,550
Company B	6,576	25	164,400
Company C	7,823	25	195,575
Company D	7,950	25	198,750
Company E	8,099	25	202,475
Company F	8,989	25	224,725
Company G	9,237	25	230,925
Company H	9,553	25	238,825
Company I	9,925	25	248,125
Company J	10,820	25	270,502
Company K	10,876	25	271,900
Company L	10,958	25	273,950
Company M	11,071	25	276,775
Company N	12,751	25	318,775

All figures based on current assumptions

$1,000,000 Death Benefit Costs
25 Payments
Female Age 55

INSURANCE COMPANY	ANNUAL PREMIUM	NUMBER OF YEARS	TOTAL PAYMENTS
Company A	$ 8,827	25	$ 220,675
Company B	9,659	25	241,475
Company C	10,491	25	262,275
Company D	10,748	25	268,700
Company E	10,796	25	269,900
Company F	12,478	25	311,950
Company G	12,483	25	312,075
Company H	12,746	25	318,650
Company I	12,972	25	324,300
Company J	13,495	25	337,375
Company K	14,424	25	360,600
Company L	14,719	25	367,975
Company M	15,076	25	376,900
Company N	16,225	25	405,625

All figures based on current assumptions

$1,000,000 Death Benefit Costs
25 Payments
Female Age 60

INSURANCE COMPANY	ANNUAL PREMIUM	NUMBER OF YEARS	TOTAL PAYMENTS
Company A	$ 12,710	25	$ 317,750
Company B	14,227	25	355,675
Company C	14,308	25	357,700
Company D	14,574	25	364,350
Company E	15,271	25	381,775
Company F	15,593	25	389,825
Company G	16,851	25	421,275
Company H	18,017	25	450,425
Company I	18,535	25	463,375
Company J	19,492	25	487,300
Company K	19,729	25	493,225
Company L	20,533	25	513,325
Company M	20,691	25	517,275
Company N	20,923	25	523,075

All figures based on current assumptions

$1,000,000 Death Benefit Costs
25 Payments
Female Age 65

INSURANCE COMPANY	ANNUAL PREMIUM	NUMBER OF YEARS	TOTAL PAYMENTS
Company A	$ 18,069	25	$ 451,725
Company B	19,650	25	491,250
Company C	20,194	25	504,850
Company D	20,757	25	518,925
Company E	20,856	25	521,400
Company F	22,345	25	558,625
Company G	22,387	25	559,675
Company H	24,980	25	624,500
Company I	25,625	25	640,625
Company J	25,978	25	649,450
Company K	26,155	25	653,875
Company L	26,999	25	674,975
Company M	27,667	25	691,675
Company N	28,077	25	701,925

All figures based on current assumptions

$1,000,000 Death Benefit Costs
25 Payments
Female Age 70

INSURANCE COMPANY	ANNUAL PREMIUM	NUMBER OF YEARS	TOTAL PAYMENTS
Company A	$ 27,276	25	$ 681,900
Company B	27,581	25	689,525
Company C	28,248	25	706,200
Company D	29,528	25	738,200
Company E	30,579	25	768,980
Company F	31,374	25	784,350
Company G	31,567	25	789,175
Company H	31,785	25	796,875
Company I	31,959	25	798,975
Company J	35,662	25	891,550
Company K	37,465	25	936,625
Company L	37,550	25	938,750
Company M	38,906	25	972,638
Company N	42,127	25	1,053,175

Death benefits can increase as payments exceed $1,000,000
All figures based on current assumptions

$1,000,000 Death Benefit Costs
25 Payments
Female Age 75

INSURANCE COMPANY	ANNUAL PREMIUM	NUMBER OF YEARS	TOTAL PAYMENTS
Company A	$ 36,627	25	$ 915,675
Company B	39,545	25	988,625
Company C	40,742	25	1,018,550
Company D	41,418	25	1,035,449
Company E	44,540	25	1,113,500
Company F	44,035	25	1,128,150
Company G	47,346	25	1,183,650
Company H	48,353	25	1,208,825
Company I	54,173	25	1,354,325
Company J	54,945	25	1,373,625
Company K	56,073	25	1,401,825
Company L	57,130	25	1,428,250
Company M	62,315	25	1,557,872
Company N	65,279	25	1,631,975

Death benefits can increase as payments exceed $1,000,000

All figures based on current assumptions

$1,000,000 Death Benefit Costs
20 Payments
Female Age 80

INSURANCE COMPANY	ANNUAL PREMIUM	NUMBER OF YEARS	TOTAL PAYMENTS
Company A	$ 59,720	20	$ 1,194,400
Company B	64,937	20	1,298,740
Company C	79,980	20	1,356,720
Company D	65,517	20	1,310,340
Company E	101,734	20	2,034,688
Company F	115,131	20	2,302,620

Death benefits can increase as payments exceed $1,000,000

All figures based on current assumptions

$1,000,000 Death Benefit Costs
One Payment
Last-To-Die
Male Age 30 / Female Age 30

INSURANCE COMPANY	ANNUAL PREMIUM	NUMBER OF YEARS	TOTAL PAYMENTS
Company A	$ 8,472	1	$ 8,472
Company B	9,006	1	9,006
Company C	10,454	1	10,454
Company D	10,980	1	10,980
Company E	15,275	1	15,275
Company F	15,349	1	15,349
Company G	22,189	1	22,189
Company H	22,797	1	22,797
Company I	24,383	1	24,383
Company J	24,731	1	24,731
Company K	25,234	1	25,234
Company L	26,250	1	26,250
Company M	26,478	1	26,478
Company N	28,375	1	28,375
Company O	28,510	1	28,510
Company P	29,369	1	29,369
Company Q	50,121	1	50,121

All figures based on current assumptions

$1,000,000 Death Benefit Costs
One Payment
Last-To-Die
Male Age 40 / Female Age 40

INSURANCE COMPANY	ANNUAL PREMIUM	NUMBER OF YEARS	TOTAL PAYMENTS
Company A	$ 18,603	1	$ 18,603
Company B	18,627	1	18,627
Company C	18,757	1	18,757
Company D	22,626	1	22,626
Company E	22,974	1	22,974
Company F	24,825	1	24,825
Company G	28,007	1	28,007
Company H	30,212	1	30,212
Company I	38,148	1	38,148
Company J	39,580	1	39,580
Company K	41,698	1	41,698
Company L	41,992	1	41,992
Company M	42,120	1	42,120
Company N	42,617	1	42,617
Company O	44,111	1	44,111
Company P	45,960	1	45,960
Company Q	44,733	1	44,733
Company R	48,769	1	48,769
Company S	49,339	1	49,339
Company T	74,195	1	74,195

All figures based on current assumptions

$1,000,000 Death Benefit Costs
One Payment
Last-To-Die
Male Age 50 / Female Age 50

INSURANCE COMPANY	ANNUAL PREMIUM	NUMBER OF YEARS	TOTAL PAYMENTS
Company A	$ 37,895	1	$ 37,895
Company B	40,508	1	40,508
Company C	40,840	1	40,840
Company D	46,445	1	46,445
Company E	48,849	1	48,849
Company F	54,723	1	54,723
Company G	55,980	1	55,980
Company H	62,147	1	62,147
Company I	67,256	1	67,256
Company J	69,545	1	69,545
Company K	71,679	1	71,679
Company L	72,157	1	72,157
Company M	72,948	1	72,948
Company N	74,638	1	74,638
Company O	79,098	1	79,098
Company P	79,114	1	79,114
Company Q	80,770	1	80,770
Company R	84,127	1	84,127
Company S	85,485	1	85,485
Company T	110,956	1	110,956

All figures based on current assumptions

$1,000,000 Death Benefit Costs
One Payment
Last-To-Die
Male Age 55 / Female Age 55

INSURANCE COMPANY	ANNUAL PREMIUM	NUMBER OF YEARS	TOTAL PAYMENTS
Company A	$ 54,504	1	$ 54,504
Company B	57,900	1	57,900
Company C	60,907	1	60,907
Company D	63,961	1	63,961
Company E	71,449	1	71,449
Company F	76,424	1	76,424
Company G	78,214	1	78,214
Company H	89,508	1	89,508
Company I	89,720	1	89,720
Company J	92,316	1	92,316
Company K	93,651	1	93,651
Company L	94,329	1	94,329
Company M	98,149	1	98,149
Company N	99,170	1	99,170
Company O	100,151	1	100,151
Company P	104,110	1	104,110
Company Q	106,499	1	106,499
Company R	111,263	1	111,263
Company S	111,732	1	111,732
Company T	137,429	1	137,429

All figures based on current assumptions

$1,000,000 Death Benefit Costs
One Payment
Last-To-Die
Male Age 60 / Female Age 60

INSURANCE COMPANY	ANNUAL PREMIUM	NUMBER OF YEARS	TOTAL PAYMENTS
Company A	$ 78,050	1	$ 78,050
Company B	82,330	1	82,330
Company C	87,526	1	87,526
Company D	99,805	1	99,805
Company E	107,722	1	107,722
Company F	108,395	1	108,395
Company G	110,487	1	110,487
Company H	118,498	1	118,498
Company I	118,862	1	118,862
Company J	121,883	1	121,883
Company K	123,199	1	123,199
Company L	126,153	1	126,153
Company M	131,932	1	131,932
Company N	134,961	1	134,961
Company O	138,378	1	138,378
Company P	139,584	1	139,584
Company Q	140,400	1	140,400
Company R	145,223	1	145,223
Company S	146,032	1	146,032
Company T	173,917	1	173,917

All figures based on current assumptions

$1,000,000 Death Benefit Costs
One Payment
Last-To-Die
Male Age 65 / Female Age 65

INSURANCE COMPANY	ANNUAL PREMIUM	NUMBER OF YEARS	TOTAL PAYMENTS
Company A	$ 112,082	1	$ 112,082
Company B	117,160	1	117,160
Company C	122,105	1	122,105
Company D	138,158	1	138,158
Company E	148,909	1	148,909
Company F	153,244	1	153,244
Company G	154,698	1	154,698
Company H	158,764	1	158,764
Company I	159,634	1	159,634
Company J	160,444	1	160,444
Company K	165,225	1	165,225
Company L	175,459	1	175,459
Company M	176,712	1	176,712
Company N	181,520	1	181,520
Company O	182,742	1	182,742
Company P	186,126	1	186,126
Company Q	191,928	1	191,928
Company R	195,110	1	195,110
Company S	199,597	1	199,597
Company T	219,759	1	219,759

All figures based on current assumptions

$1,000,000 Death Benefit Costs
One Payment
Last-To-Die
Male Age 70 / Female Age 70

INSURANCE COMPANY	ANNUAL PREMIUM	NUMBER OF YEARS	TOTAL PAYMENTS
Company A	$ 158,752	1	$ 158,752
Company B	160,553	1	160,553
Company C	166,693	1	166,693
Company D	188,945	1	188,945
Company E	207,814	1	207,814
Company F	214,904	1	214,904
Company G	224,224	1	224,224
Company H	224,486	1	224,486
Company I	228,113	1	228,113
Company J	234,675	1	234,675
Company K	236,767	1	236,767
Company L	239,350	1	239,350
Company M	248,468	1	248,468
Company N	257,169	1	257,169
Company O	260,686	1	260,686
Company P	275,460	1	275,460
Company Q	277,928	1	277,928
Company R	279,018	1	279,018

All figures based on current assumptions

$1,000,000 Death Benefit Costs
One Payment
Last-To-Die
Male Age 75 / Female Age 75

INSURANCE COMPANY	ANNUAL PREMIUM	NUMBER OF YEARS	TOTAL PAYMENTS
Company A	$ 205,031	1	$ 205,031
Company B	217,119	1	217,119
Company C	231,467	1	231,467
Company D	254,211	1	254,211
Company E	286,176	1	286,176
Company F	295,572	1	295,572
Company G	296,261	1	296,261
Company H	318,477	1	318,477
Company I	318,857	1	318,857
Company J	323,859	1	323,859
Company K	328,881	1	328,881
Company L	336,514	1	336,514
Company M	349,185	1	349,185
Company N	354,710	1	354,710
Company O	364,960	1	364,960
Company P	378,791	1	378,791
Company Q	387,909	1	387,909
Company R	399,100	1	399,100
Company S	475,080	1	475,080

All figures based on current assumptions

$1,000,000 Death Benefit Costs
One Payment
Last-To-Die
Male Age 80 / Female Age 80

INSURANCE COMPANY	ANNUAL PREMIUM	NUMBER OF YEARS	TOTAL PAYMENTS
Company A	$ 292,856	1	$ 292,856
Company B	315,976	1	315,976
Company C	393,887	1	393,887
Company D	398,857	1	398,857
Company E	417,620	1	417,620
Company F	450,460	1	450,460
Company G	453,363	1	453,363
Company H	494,750	1	494,750
Company I	505,734	1	505,734
Company J	525,826	1	525,826
Company K	568,390	1	568,390
Company L	612,792	1	612,792

All figures based on current assumptions

$1,000,000 Death Benefit Costs
Limited Payments
Last-To-Die
Male Age 30 / Female Age 30

INSURANCE COMPANY	ANNUAL PREMIUM	NUMBER OF YEARS	TOTAL PAYMENTS
Company A	$ 1,269	8	$ 10,154
Company B	1,622	7	11,354
Company C	2,033	6	12,210
Company D	1,987	7	13,910
Company E	1,795	8	14,360
Company F	3,695	5	16,023
Company G	2,501	8	20,008
Company H	3,590	7	25,130
Company I	5,881	5	29,406
Company J	3,765	8	30,120
Company K	4,472	7	31,304
Company L	4,740	7	32,283
Company M	3,620	9	32,580
Company N	3,715	9	32,666
Company O	3,390	10	33,900
Company P	3,819	10	38,190
Company Q	4,110	10	40,301
Company R	3,510	12	42,120
Company S	6,541	11	71,951

All figures based on current assumptions

$1,000,000 Death Benefit Costs
Limited Payments
Last-To-Die
Male Age 40 / Female Age 40

INSURANCE COMPANY	ANNUAL PREMIUM	NUMBER OF YEARS	TOTAL PAYMENTS
Company A	$ 3,354	7	$ 23,478
Company B	3,085	8	24,680
Company C	3,184	8	25,472
Company D	4,188	7	29,319
Company E	5,310	5	26,550
Company F	5,027	6	30,162
Company G	7,175	5	31,611
Company H	4,586	8	36,688
Company I	6,270	6	37,620
Company J	9,563	5	47,817
Company K	7,444	7	52,108
Company L	6,535	8	52,280
Company M	6,870	8	54,961
Company N	5,755	10	57,550
Company O	6,430	9	57,870
Company P	6,000	10	60,000
Company Q	5,355	12	64,260
Company R	5,960	11	65,560
Company S	6,567	10	65,670
Company T	6,644	10	66,440
Company U	9,830	11	108,130

All figures based on current assumptions

$1,000,000 Death Benefit Costs
Limited Payments
Last-To-Die
Male Age 50 / Female Age 50

INSURANCE COMPANY	ANNUAL PREMIUM	NUMBER OF YEARS	TOTAL PAYMENTS
Company A	$ 7,294	7	$ 51,058
Company B	6,483	8	51,864
Company C	6,886	8	55,088
Company D	9,440	6	56,640
Company E	8,961	7	62,727
Company F	10,681	6	64,090
Company G	11,565	6	68,025
Company H	11,609	6	69,054
Company I	8,960	8	71,680
Company J	16,202	5	81,008
Company K	12,684	7	88,788
Company L	11,420	8	91,360
Company M	11,635	8	93,080
Company N	11,845	8	97,760
Company O	11,153	9	100,377
Company P	10,770	10	107,700
Company Q	10,484	10	104,840
Company R	11,315	10	113,150
Company S	11,353	10	113,530
Company T	10,335	11	113,685
Company U	14,885	11	167,735

All figures based on current assumptions

$1,000,000 Death Benefit Costs
Limited Payments
Last-To-Die
Male Age 55 / Female Age 55

INSURANCE COMPANY	ANNUAL PREMIUM	NUMBER OF YEARS	TOTAL PAYMENTS
Company A	$ 10,426	7	$ 72,982
Company B	9,326	8	74,608
Company C	13,000	6	78,000
Company D	10,274	8	82,192
Company E	13,108	7	91,756
Company F	13,132	7	91,930
Company G	16,083	6	96,498
Company H	12,513	8	100,104
Company I	14,955	7	101,098
Company J	21,164	5	105,818
Company K	16,553	7	115,871
Company L	15,170	8	121,360
Company M	15,725	8	125,800
Company N	14,362	9	129,258
Company O	13,566	10	135,660
Company P	15,089	9	135,801
Company Q	14,170	10	141,700
Company R	16,223	9	146,007
Company S	14,962	10	149,620
Company T	13,955	11	153,505
Company U	19,069	10	190,690

All figures based on current assumptions

$1,000,000 Death Benefit Costs
Limited Payments
Last-To-Die
Male Age 60 / Female Age 60

INSURANCE COMPANY	ANNUAL PREMIUM	NUMBER OF YEARS	TOTAL PAYMENTS
Company A	$ 14,867	7	$ 104,069
Company B	13,357	8	106,856
Company C	14,783	8	118,264
Company D	18,060	7	126,420
Company E	22,158	6	132,954
Company F	19,421	7	135,950
Company G	27,295	5	136,477
Company H	20,280	7	141,960
Company I	17,760	8	142,080
Company J	19,695	9	145,213
Company K	20,919	7	146,433
Company L	20,120	8	160,960
Company M	21,515	8	172,120
Company N	19,773	9	177,957
Company O	19,845	9	178,605
Company P	18,242	10	182,420
Company Q	20,400	9	183,600
Company R	18,545	10	185,450
Company S	23,695	9	186,255
Company T	19,498	10	194,980
Company U	25,261	9	227,349

All figures based on current assumptions

$1,000,000 Death Benefit Costs
Limited Payments
Last-To-Die
Male Age 65 / Female Age 65

INSURANCE COMPANY	ANNUAL PREMIUM	NUMBER OF YEARS	TOTAL PAYMENTS
Company A	$ 21,240	7	$ 148,680
Company B	19,187	8	153,496
Company C	20,616	8	164,928
Company D	25,000	7	175,000
Company E	35,836	5	179,180
Company F	30,656	6	183,936
Company G	24,206	8	193,650
Company H	27,946	7	195,622
Company I	28,395	7	198,765
Company J	25,141	8	201,128
Company K	26,780	8	214,240
Company L	26,665	9	221,469
Company M	25,319	9	227,871
Company N	26,200	9	235,800
Company O	29,835	8	238,680
Company P	30,110	8	240,880
Company Q	26,766	9	240,894
Company R	24,335	10	243,350
Company S	31,531	8	252,248
Company T	25,693	10	256,930
Company U	34,063	8	272,504

All figures based on current assumptions

$1,000,000 Death Benefit Costs
Limited Payments
Last-To-Die
Male Age 70 / Female Age 70

INSURANCE COMPANY	ANNUAL PREMIUM	NUMBER OF YEARS	TOTAL PAYMENTS
Company A	$ 30,438	7	$ 213,066
Company B	27,136	8	217,088
Company C	27,204	8	217,632
Company D	34,190	7	239,330
Company E	49,974	5	249,870
Company F	42,867	6	257,202
Company G	39,497	7	276,479
Company H	36,023	8	288,184
Company I	37,160	8	297,280
Company J	34,392	9	309,528
Company K	30,955	10	309,550
Company L	35,655	9	313,496
Company M	46,115	7	322,805
Company N	35,983	9	323,847
Company O	32,529	10	325,290
Company P	46,921	7	328,447
Company Q	37,050	9	333,450
Company R	42,055	8	336,440
Company S	45,326	8	362,608
Company T	45,460	8	363,680
Company U	37,019	10	370,190

All figures based on current assumptions

$1,000,000 Death Benefit Costs
Limited Payments
Last-To-Die
Male Age 75 / Female Age 75

INSURANCE COMPANY	ANNUAL PREMIUM	NUMBER OF YEARS	TOTAL PAYMENTS
Company A	$ 34,761	8	$ 278,088
Company B	37,230	8	297,840
Company C	42,806	7	299,642
Company D	46,000	7	322,000
Company E	70,853	5	354,266
Company F	59,343	6	356,058
Company G	54,659	7	382,613
Company H	48,919	8	391,352
Company I	49,309	8	394,472
Company J	47,974	9	431,766
Company K	45,655	10	456,550
Company L	52,030	9	468,270
Company M	53,245	9	475,470
Company N	59,960	8	479,680
Company O	60,235	8	481,880
Company P	44,706	11	491,766
Company Q	51,358	10	513,580
Company R	66,202	8	529,616
Company S	66,300	9	558,597
Company T	84,089	7	588,623

All figures based on current assumptions

$1,000,000 Death Benefit Costs
Limited Payments
Last-To-Die
Male Age 80 / Female Age 80

INSURANCE COMPANY	ANNUAL PREMIUM	NUMBER OF YEARS	TOTAL PAYMENTS
Company A	$ 50,376	8	$ 403,008
Company B	59,721	7	418,047
Company C	80,722	6	496,332
Company D	100,378	5	501,890
Company E	74,272	7	519,904
Company F	67,556	8	540,448
Company G	69,710	8	557,680
Company H	61,528	9	553,752
Company I	69,409	10	694,090
Company J	63,447	11	697,925
Company K	87,285	8	698,280
Company L	93,390	8	747,120
Company M	95,184	8	761,472

All figures based on current assumptions

$1,000,000 Death Benefit Costs
25 Payments
Last-To-Die
Male Age 30 / Female Age 30

INSURANCE COMPANY	ANNUAL PREMIUM	NUMBER OF YEARS	TOTAL PAYMENTS
Company A	$ 517	25	$ 12,925
Company B	532	25	13,302
Company C	953	25	23,828
Company D	1,020	25	25,514
Company E	1,382	25	34,550
Company F	2,298	25	57,450
Company G	2,759	25	68,975
Company H	3,316	25	82,900
Company I	3,320	25	83,000
Company J	3,518	25	87,950
Company K	3,655	25	91,375
Company L	4,740	25	118,500

All figures based on current assumptions

$1,000,000 Death Benefit Costs
25 Payments
Last-To-Die
Male Age 40 / Female Age 40

INSURANCE COMPANY	ANNUAL PREMIUM	NUMBER OF YEARS	TOTAL PAYMENTS
Company A	$ 1,504	25	$ 37,600
Company B	1,745	25	43,623
Company C	1.857	25	46,444
Company D	2,031	25	50,793
Company E	2,535	25	63,375
Company F	2,559	25	63,966
Company G	4,717	25	117,925
Company H	4,975	25	124,375
Company I	5,248	25	131,200
Company J	5,310	25	132,750
Company K	5,424	25	135,600
Company L	6,335	25	158,375
Company M	7,560	25	189,000

All figures based on current assumptions

$1,000,000 Death Benefit Costs
25 Payments
Last-To-Die
Male Age 50 / Female Age 50

INSURANCE COMPANY	ANNUAL PREMIUM	NUMBER OF YEARS	TOTAL PAYMENTS
Company A	$ 3,527	25	$ 88,185
Company B	3,802	25	95,050
Company C	4,564	25	114,115
Company D	4,924	25	123,091
Company E	4,960	25	124,000
Company F	4,984	25	124,598
Company G	7,520	25	188,000
Company H	8,206	25	205,150
Company I	8,617	25	215,425
Company J	9,160	25	229,000
Company K	9,440	25	236,000
Company L	11,165	25	279,125
Company M	12,340	25	308,500

All figures based on current assumptions

$1,000,000 Death Benefit Costs
25 Payments
Last-To-Die
Male Age 55 / Female Age 55

INSURANCE COMPANY	ANNUAL PREMIUM	NUMBER OF YEARS	TOTAL PAYMENTS
Company A	$ 4,809	25	$ 120,225
Company B	5,289	25	132,223
Company C	5,482	25	137,050
Company D	6,492	25	162,295
Company E	6,942	25	173,550
Company F	7,128	25	178,191
Company G	7,425	25	185,621
Company H	9,631	25	240,775
Company I	10,910	25	272,750
Company J	11,498	25	287,450
Company K	12,092	25	302,300
Company L	13,000	25	325,000
Company M	14,925	25	373,125
Company N	16,000	25	400,000

All figures based on current assumptions

$1,000,000 Death Benefit Costs
25 Payments
Last-To-Die
Male Age 60 / Female Age 60

INSURANCE COMPANY	ANNUAL PREMIUM	NUMBER OF YEARS	TOTAL PAYMENTS
Company A	$ 7,012	25	$ 175,300
Company B	7,657	25	191,419
Company C	7,891	25	197,275
Company D	9,923	25	248,075
Company E	10,063	25	251,575
Company F	10,251	25	256,282
Company G	10,558	25	263,950
Company H	13,844	25	346,100
Company I	14,590	25	364,750
Company J	15,835	25	395,875
Company K	15,894	25	397,350
Company L	18,060	25	451,500
Company M	20,085	25	502,125
Company N	20,550	25	513,750

All figures based on current assumptions

$1,000,000 Death Benefit Costs
25 Payments
Last-To-Die
Male Age 65 / Female Age 65

INSURANCE COMPANY	ANNUAL PREMIUM	NUMBER OF YEARS	TOTAL PAYMENTS
Company A	$ 10,360	25	$ 259,000
Company B	11,026	25	275,650
Company C	11,454	25	286,350
Company D	14,080	25	351,990
Company E	14,331	25	358,275
Company F	14,567	25	364,176
Company G	14,949	25	373,725
Company H	18,902	25	472,550
Company I	19,863	25	496,575
Company J	21,004	25	525,100
Company K	22,597	25	564,925
Company L	25,000	25	625,000
Company M	26,460	25	661,500
Company N	27,115	25	667,875

All figures based on current assumptions

$1,000,000 Death Benefit Costs
25 Payments
Last-To-Die
Male Age 70 / Female Age 70

INSURANCE COMPANY	ANNUAL PREMIUM	NUMBER OF YEARS	TOTAL PAYMENTS
Company A	$ 15,038	25	$ 375,959
Company B	15,587	25	389,675
Company C	16,537	25	413,440
Company D	19,446	25	486,146
Company E	20,785	25	519,644
Company F	21,791	25	544,775
Company G	27,258	25	681,450
Company H	27,912	25	697,800
Company I	28,430	25	710,750
Company J	33,282	25	832,050
Company K	34,190	25	854,750
Company L	35,050	25	876,250
Company M	36,865	25	921,625

All figures based on current assumptions

$1,000,000 Death Benefit Costs
25 Payments
Last-To-Die
Male Age 75 / Female Age 75

INSURANCE COMPANY	ANNUAL PREMIUM	NUMBER OF YEARS	TOTAL PAYMENTS
Company A	$ 20,091	25	$ 502,244
Company B	23,395	25	584,875
Company C	23,480	25	587,000
Company D	25,442	25	636,052
Company E	30,667	25	766,671
Company F	31,541	25	788,525
Company G	32,858	25	821,450
Company H	39,474	25	986,850
Company I	40,566	25	1,014,150
Company J	41,688	25	1,042,200
Company K	46,000	25	1,150,000
Company L	47,850	25	1,196,250
Company M	50,076	25	1,251,900
Company N	50,285	25	1,257,125

Death benefits can increase as payments exceed $1,000,000
All figures based on current assumptions

$1,000,000 Death Benefit Costs
20 Payments
Last-To-Die
Male Age 80 / Female Age 80

INSURANCE COMPANY	ANNUAL PREMIUM	NUMBER OF YEARS	TOTAL PAYMENTS
Company A	$ 31,487	20	$ 629,738
Company B	33,925	20	678,500
Company C	35,546	20	710,920
Company D	47,731	15	715,967
Company E	52,067	20	1,041,340
Company F	57,238	20	1,144,760
Company G	65,138	20	1,302,760
Company H	65,830	20	1,316,600
Company I	68,455	20	1,369,100
Company J	68,890	20	1,377,800

Death benefits can increase as payments exceed $1,000,000
All figures based on current assumptions

Appendix

The High Cost of Dying

The Estimated Cost of Settling an Estate

The Following Table Assumes the "Last-To-Die"
Spouse Leaves the Remaining Estate Assets
to the Children or Any Other Person(s).

TOTAL TAXABLE ESTATE	STATUTORY PROBATE FEES**	APPROXIMATE FEDERAL TAX	ESTATE EXPENSES (TOTAL OF COL. 2&3)	% OF TAXABLE ESTATE (COL. 1)	% OF INCREASE FOR NEXT PORTION OF REMAINING TAXABLE ESTATE
(1)	(2)	(3)	(4)	(5)	(6)
$ 600,000	$ 26,300	$ 0	$ 26,300	4.4	37.0
1,000,000	42,300	153,000	195,300	37.7	44.0
1,500,000	52,300	363,000	415,300	39.5	47.0
2,000,000	62,300	588,000	650,300	41.4	53.0
3,000,000	82,300	1,098,000	1,180,300	44.2	55.0
4,000,000	102,300	1,648,000	1,750,300	46.9	55.0
5,000,000	122,300	2,198,000	2,320,300	47.9	55.0
7,500,000	172,300	3,573,000	3,745,300	49.9	55.0
10,000,000*	222,300	4,948,000	5,170,300	49.9	55.0
20,000,000*	422,300	10,948,000	11,370,300	56.9	55.0
30,000,000*	622,300	16,500,000	17,122,300	57.1	55.0
40,000,000*	822,300	22,000,000	22,822,300	57.1	55.0
50,000,000*	1,022,300	27,500,000	28,522,300	57.0	55.0
100,000,000*	2,044,300	55,000,000	57,044,300	57.0	55.0

* The $600,000 exemption is lost for estate over $10,000,000.
** A combination of court costs plus attorney fees that are established by statute.
These are the minimum costs; however, it is very unusual for an estate to be settled
at such a low cost. Extraordinary fees are added for time delays, disputes, ap-
praisals, sales of assets, and many other items. Average probate fees are much
higher than shown.

Form **706**

(Rev. October 1988)

Department of the Treasury
Internal Revenue Service

United States Estate (and Generation-Skipping Transfer) Tax Return

Estate of a citizen or resident of the United States (see separate instructions). To be filed for decedents dying after October 22, 1986, and before January 1, 1990.
For Paperwork Reduction Act Notice, see page 1 of the instructions.

OMB No. 1545-0015
Expires 8-30-91

Part 1.—Decedent and Executor

1a Decedent's first name and middle initial (and maiden name, if any)	1b Decedent's last name	2 Decedent's social security no.

3a Domicile at time of death	3b Year domicile established	4 Date of birth	5 Date of death

6a Name of executor (see instructions)	6b Executor's address (number and street including apartment number or rural route; city, town, or post office; state; and ZIP code)

6c Executor's social security number (see instructions)

7a Name and location of court where will was probated or estate administered	7b Case number

8 If decedent died testate, check here ▶ ☐ and attach a certified copy of the will.   9 If Form 4768 is attached, check here ▶ ☐

10 If Schedule R-1 is attached, check here ▶ ☐   *See page 2 for representative's authorization.*

Part 2.—Tax Computation

1	Total gross estate (from Part 5, Recapitulation, page 3, item 10).	1
2	Total allowable deductions (from Part 5, Recapitulation, page 3, item 25)	2
3	Taxable estate (subtract line 2 from line 1)	3
4	Adjusted taxable gifts (total taxable gifts (within the meaning of section 2503) made by the decedent after December 31, 1976, other than gifts that are includible in decedent's gross estate (section 2001(b))). . .	4
5	Add lines 3 and 4	5
6	Tentative tax on the amount on line 5 from Table A in the instructions	6
	Note: *If decedent died before January 1, 1988, skip lines 7a-c and enter the amount from line 6 on line 8.*	

7a If line 5 exceeds $10,000,000, enter the lesser of line 5 or $21,040,000. If line 5 is $10,000,000 or less, skip lines 7a and 7b and enter zero on line 7c | 7a |

   b Subtract $10,000,000 from line 7a . . . . | 7b |

c	Enter 5% (.05) of line 7b	7c
8	Total tentative tax (add lines 6 and 7c)	8
9	Total gift tax payable with respect to gifts made by the decedent after December 31, 1976. Include gift taxes paid by the decedent's spouse for split gifts (section 2513) only if the decedent was the donor of these gifts and they are includible in the decedent's gross estate (see instructions)	9
10	Gross estate tax (subtract line 9 from line 8)	10
11	Unified credit against estate tax from Table B in the instructions 11	
12	Adjustment to unified credit. (This adjustment may not exceed $6,000. See instructions.) 12	
13	Allowable unified credit (subtract line 12 from line 11)	13
14	Subtract line 13 from line 10 (but do not enter less than zero)	14
15	Credit for state death taxes. Do not enter more than line 14. Compute credit by using amount on line 3 less $60,000. See Table C in the instructions and **attach credit evidence** (see instructions)	15
16	Subtract line 15 from line 14	16
17	Credit for Federal gift taxes on pre-1977 gifts (section 2012)(attach computation) 17	
18	Credit for foreign death taxes (from Schedule(s) P). (Attach Form(s) 706CE) 18	
19	Credit for tax on prior transfers (from Schedule Q) 19	
20	Total (add lines 17, 18, and 19)	20
21	Net estate tax (subtract line 20 from line 16)	21
22	Generation-skipping transfer taxes (from Schedule R, Part 2, line 12)	22
23	Section 4980A increased estate tax (attach Schedule S (Form 706)) (see instructions)	23
24	Total transfer taxes (add lines 21, 22, and 23)	24
25	Prior payments. Explain in an attached statement 25	
26	United States Treasury bonds redeemed in payment of estate tax . . . 26	
27	Total (add lines 25 and 26)	27
28	Balance due (subtract line 27 from line 24)	28

Under penalties of perjury, I declare that I have examined this return, including accompanying schedules and statements, and to the best of my knowledge and belief, it is true, correct, and complete. Declaration of preparer other than the executor is based on all information of which preparer has any knowledge.

Signature(s) of executor(s)   Date

Signature of preparer other than executor   Address (and ZIP code)   Date

Department of the Treasury
Internal Revenue Service

Instructions for Form 706

(Revised October 1988)
United States Estate (and Generation-Skipping Transfer) Tax Return

(Section references are to the Internal Revenue Code unless otherwise noted.)

Paperwork Reduction Act Notice.—
We ask for this information to carry out the Internal Revenue laws of the United States. We need it to ensure that you are complying with these laws and to allow us to figure and collect the right amount of tax. You are required to give us this information.

The time needed to complete and file this form will vary depending on individual circumstances. The estimated average time is:

Recordkeeping . . . . . 6 hrs., 59 min.
Learning about the law or the form . . . . . 4 hrs., 3 min.
Preparing the form . . . 6 hrs., 12 min.
Copying, assembling, and sending the form to IRS . 4 hrs., 12 min.

If you have comments concerning the accuracy of these time estimates or suggestions for making this form more simple, we would be happy to hear from you. You can write to the **Internal Revenue Service**, Washington, DC 20224, Attention: IRS Reports Clearance Officer, TR:FP; or the **Office of Management and Budget,** Paperwork Reduction Project, Washington, DC 20503.

Changes You Should Note

● The scheduled decline in estate tax rates is deferred until 1993.
● The benefit of the unified credit and graduated rates is phased out for transfers exceeding $10 million for decedents dying after 1987.
● Transfers of a disproportionate share of the potential appreciation in an enterprise may be includible in the gross estate of decedents dying after 1987 for property transferred after December 17, 1987.
● The rules relating to the sale of employer securities to an employee stock ownership plan or an eligible worker-owned cooperative are clarified, and new limits on the deduction have been added. The sale is reported on Schedule N. The new limits are computed on lines 21–24 of the Recapitulation.
● The Power of Attorney authorization has been moved to Part 4 on page 2.

Purpose of Form

The executor of a decedent's estate uses Form 706 to figure the estate tax imposed by Chapter 11 of the Internal Revenue Code. This tax is levied on the entire taxable estate, not just on the share received by a particular beneficiary. Form 706 is also used to compute the Generation-Skipping Transfer (GST) tax imposed by Chapter 13 on direct skips (transfers to skip persons of interests in property included in the decedent's gross estate).

Which Estates Must File

Form 706 must be filed by the executor for the estate of every U.S. citizen or resident whose gross estate, plus adjusted taxable gifts and specific exemption, is more than certain limitations.

To determine whether you must file a return for the estate add:

(1) The adjusted taxable gifts (under section 2001(b)) made by the decedent after December 31, 1976; and

(2) The total specific exemption allowed under section 2521 (as in effect before its repeal by the Tax Reform Act of 1976) with respect to gifts made by the decedent after September 8, 1976; and

(3) The decedent's gross estate **valued at the date of death.**

You must file a return for the estate if the total of (1), (2) and (3) above is more than $500,000 for decedents dying in 1986, or $600,000 for decedents dying after 1986. For filing requirements for decedents dying after 1981 and before 1986, see the November 1987 Revision of Form 706.

Gross estate.—The gross estate includes all property in which the decedent had an interest (including real property outside the United States). It also includes:

● Certain transfers made during the decedent's life without an adequate and full consideration in money or money's worth;
● Annuities;
● Joint estates with right of survivorship;
● Tenancies by the entirety;
● Life insurance proceeds (even though payable to beneficiaries other than the estate);
● Property over which the decedent possessed a general power of appointment;
● Dower or curtesy (or statutory estate) of the surviving spouse;
● Community property to the extent of the decedent's interest as defined by applicable law.

For more specific information, see the instructions to Schedules A through I.

U.S. Citizens or Residents; Nonresident Noncitizens

File Form 706 for the estates of decedents who were either U.S. citizens or U.S. residents at the time of death. File **Form 706NA,** United States Estate (and Generation-Skipping Transfer) Tax Return, Estate of nonresident not a citizen of the United States, for the estates of nonresident alien decedents (decedents who were neither U.S. citizens nor residents at the time of death).

Residents of U.S. possessions.—All references to citizens of the United States are subject to the provisions of sections 2208 and 2209, relating to decedents who were U.S. citizens and residents of a U.S. possession on the date of death. If such a decedent became a U.S. citizen only because of his or her connection with a possession, then the decedent is considered a nonresident alien decedent for estate tax purposes, and you should file Form 706NA. If such a decedent became a U.S. citizen wholly independently of his or her connection with a possession, then the decedent is considered a U.S. citizen for estate tax purposes, and you should file Form 706.

Executor.—"Executor" means the executor, personal representative, or administrator of the decedent's estate. If none of these is appointed, qualified, and acting in the United States, every person in actual or constructive possession of any property of the decedent is considered an executor and must file a return.

When To File

You must file Form 706 to report estate and/or Generation-Skipping Transfer tax within 9 months after the date of the decedent's death unless you receive an extension of time for filing. Use **Form 4768,** Application for Extension of Time to File, to apply for an extension of time. If you received an extension, attach a copy of it to Form 706.

Where To File

Unless the return is hand carried to the office of the District Director, please mail it to the Internal Revenue Service Center indicated below for the state where the decedent was domiciled at the time of death. If you are filing a return for the estate of a nonresident citizen, mail it to the Internal Revenue Service Center, Philadelphia, PA 19255, USA.

Alabama*, Florida, Georgia, Mississippi*, South Carolina	Atlanta, GA 31101
New Jersey, New York City and counties of Nassau, Rockland, Suffolk, and Westchester	Holtsville, NY 00501
New York (all other counties), Connecticut, Maine, Massachusetts, Minnesota*, New Hampshire, Rhode Island, Vermont	Andover, MA 05501
Illinois, Iowa, Minnesota**, Missouri, Wisconsin	Kansas City, MO 64999
Delaware, District of Columbia, Maryland, Pennsylvania, Virginia**	Philadelphia, PA 19255
Indiana**, Kentucky, Michigan, Ohio, West Virginia	Cincinnati, OH 45999
Kansas, Louisiana, New Mexico, Oklahoma, Texas	Austin, TX 73301

[¶ 157]   *(continued on page 2)*

For a complete 706 form contact the Internal Revenue Service

**Department of the Treasury
Internal Revenue Service**

Instructions for Form 709

(Revised December 1989)

United States Gift (and Generation-Skipping Transfer) Tax Return

(For gifts made after December 31, 1988, and before January 1, 1990)
For Privacy Act Notice, see the Instructions for Form 1040
(Section references are to the Internal Revenue Code unless otherwise noted.)

If you are filing this form solely to elect gift-splitting for gifts of not more than $20,000 per donee, you may be able to use Form 709-A, United States Short Form Gift Tax Return, instead of this form. See the Instructions for "Who Must File" on page 2.

If you made gifts before January 1, 1982, do not use this Form 709 to report these gifts. Instead, use the November 1981 revision of Form 709. For gifts made after December 31, 1981, and before January 1, 1987, use the January 1987 revision of Form 709. For gifts made after December 31, 1986, and before January 1, 1989, use the December 1988 revision of Form 709.

Paperwork Reduction Act Notice.—We ask for this information to carry out the Internal Revenue laws of the United States. We need it to ensure that taxpayers are complying with these laws and to allow us to figure and collect the right amount of tax. You are required to give us this information.

The time needed to complete and file this form will vary depending on individual circumstances. The estimated average time is:

Recordkeeping	40 min.
Learning about the law or the form	54 min.
Preparing the form	1 hr., 52 min.
Copying, assembling, and sending the form to IRS	1 hr., 3 min.

If you have comments concerning the accuracy of these time estimates or suggestions for making this form more simple, we would be happy to hear from you. You can write to the **Internal Revenue Service,** Washington, DC 20224, Attention: IRS Reports Clearance Officer, T:FP; or the **Office of Management and Budget,** Paperwork Reduction Project (1545-0020), Washington, DC 20503.

General Instructions

Purpose of Form.—Form 709 is used to report transfers subject to the Federal gift and certain generation-skipping (GST) taxes and to figure the tax, if any, due on those transfers.

All gift and GST taxes are computed and filed on a calendar year basis regardless of your income tax accounting period.

Transfers Subject to the Gift Tax.—Generally, the Federal gift tax applies to any transfer by gift of real or personal property, whether tangible or intangible, that you made directly or indirectly, in trust, or by any other means to a donee.

The gift tax applies not only to the gratuitous transfer of any kind of property, but also to sales or exchanges, not made in the ordinary course of business, where money or money's worth is exchanged but the value of the money received is less than the value of what is sold or exchanged. The gift tax is in addition to any other tax, such as Federal income tax, paid or due on the transfer.

The exercise or release of a power of appointment may be a gift by the individual possessing the power.

The gift tax may also apply to the forgiveness of a debt, to interest-free (or below market interest rate) loans, to the assignment of the benefits of an insurance policy, to certain property settlements in divorce cases, and to certain survivorship annuities.

A gift may also occur when a transfer is subject to the asset valuation freeze rules of section 2036(c)(1). If, before the death of the original transferor, either:

1. the original transferor transfers all or any portion of the retained interest, or

2. the original transferee transfers all or any portion of the transferred property to a person who is not a member of the original transferor's family,

then the original transferor will be treated as having made a gift to the original transferee. For definitions and additional details of this type of transfer, see section 2036(c) and the instructions for Schedule G of Form 706.

Bonds that are exempt from Federal income taxes are not exempt from Federal gift taxes.

Pub. 448, Federal Estate and Gift Taxes, contains further information on the gift tax.

Transfers Not Subject to the Gift Tax.—Three types of transfers are not subject to the gift tax. These are transfers to political organizations and payments that qualify for the educational and medical exclusions. These transfers are not "gifts" as that term is used on Form 709 and its instructions. You need not file a Form 709 to report these transfers and should not list them on Schedule A of Form 709.

Political organizations.—The gift tax does not apply to a gift to a political organization (defined in section 527(e)(1)) for the use of the organization.

Educational exclusion.—The gift tax does not apply to an amount you paid on behalf of an individual to a qualifying domestic or foreign educational organization as tuition for the education or training of the individual. A *qualifying educational organization* is one that normally maintains a regular faculty and curriculum and normally has a regularly enrolled body of pupils or students in attendance at the place where its educational activities are regularly carried on. See section 170(b)(1)(A)(ii) and its regulations.

The payment must be made directly to the qualifying educational organization and it must be for tuition. No educational exclusion is allowed for amounts paid for books, supplies, dormitory fees, board or other similar expenses that do not constitute direct tuition costs. To the extent that the payment to the educational institution was for something other than tuition, it is a gift to the individual for whose benefit it was made, and may be offset by the annual exclusion if it is otherwise available.

Medical exclusion.—The gift tax does not apply to an amount you paid on behalf of an individual to a person or institution that provided medical care for the individual. The payment must be to the care provider. The medical care must meet the requirements of section 213(d) (definition of medical care for income tax deduction purposes). Medical care includes expenses incurred for the diagnosis, cure, mitigation, treatment, or prevention of disease, or for the purpose of affecting any structure or function of the body, or for transportation primarily for and essential to medical care. Medical care also includes amounts paid for medical insurance on behalf of any individual.

Form **709**

(Rev. January 1987)

Department of the Treasury
Internal Revenue Service

United States Gift (and Generation-Skipping Transfer) Tax Return

(Section 6019 of the Internal Revenue Code) (For gifts made after December 31, 1981, and before January 1, 1989)

Calendar year 19 _____

► **For Privacy Act Notice, see the Instructions for Form 1040.**

OMB No. 1545-0020
Expires 12-31-89

Part 1.—General Information

1 Donor's first name and middle initial	2 Donor's last name	3 Social security number
4 Address (number and street)		5 Domicile
6 City, state, and ZIP code		7 Citizenship

	Yes	No
8 If the donor died during the year, check here ► ☐ and enter date of death ______________, 19 _____.		
9 If you received an extension of time to file this Form 709, check here ►☐ and attach the Form 4868, 2688, 2350, or extension letter.		
10 If you (the donor) filed a previous Form 709 (or 709-A), has your address changed since the last Form 709 (or 709-A) was filed?		
11 Gifts by husband or wife to third parties.—Do you consent to have the gifts (including generation-skipping transfers) made by you and by your spouse to third parties during the calendar year considered as made one-half by each of you? (See instructions.)		
(If the answer is "Yes," the following information must be furnished and your spouse is to sign the consent shown below. If the answer is "No," skip lines 12–17 and go to Schedule A.)		
12 Name of consenting spouse — 13 Social security number		
14 Were you married to one another during the entire calendar year? (See instructions.)		
15 If the answer to 14 is "No," check whether ☐ married ☐ divorced or ☐ widowed, and give date (see instructions) ►		
16 Will a gift tax return for this calendar year be filed by your spouse?		

17 **Consent of Spouse**—I consent to have the gifts (and generation-skipping transfers) made by me and by my spouse to third parties during the calendar year considered as made one-half by each of us. We are both aware of the joint and several liability for tax created by the execution of this consent.

Consenting spouse's signature ► **Date** ►

Part 2.—Tax Computation

1	Enter the amount from Schedule A, line 15	1	
2	Enter the amount from Schedule B, line 3	2	
3	Total taxable gifts (add lines 1 and 2)	3	
4	Tax computed on amount on line 3 (see Table A for the current year in separate instructions)	4	
5	Tax computed on amount on line 2 (see Table A for the current year in separate instructions)	5	
6	Balance (subtract line 5 from line 4)	6	
7	Enter the unified credit from Table B (see instructions)	7	
8	Enter the unified credit against tax allowable for all prior periods (from Sch. B, line 1, col. (c))	8	
9	Balance (subtract line 8 from line 7)	9	
10	Enter 20% of the amount allowed as a specific exemption for gifts made after September 8, 1976, and before January 1, 1977 (see instructions)	10	
11	Balance (subtract line 10 from line 9)	11	
12	Unified credit (enter the smaller of line 6 or line 11)	12	
13	Credit for foreign gift taxes (see instructions)	13	
14	Total credits (add lines 12 and 13)	14	
15	Balance (subtract line 14 from line 6) (do not enter less than zero)	15	
16	Generation-skipping transfer taxes (from Schedule C, Part 4, col. H, total)	16	
17	Total taxes (add lines 15 and 16)	17	
18	Gift and generation-skipping transfer taxes prepaid with extension of time to file	18	
19	If line 18 is less than line 17, enter BALANCE DUE (see instructions)	19	
20	If line 18 is greater than line 17, enter AMOUNT TO BE REFUNDED	20	

Please attach check or money order here

Please attach the necessary supplemental documents; see instructions.

Under penalties of perjury, I declare that I have examined this return, including any accompanying schedules and statements, and to the best of my knowledge and belief it is true, correct, and complete. Declaration of preparer (other than donor) is based on all information of which preparer has any knowledge.

Donor's signature ► Date ►

Preparer's signature (other than donor) ► Date ►

Preparer's address (other than donor) ►

For Paperwork Reduction Act Notice, see page 1 of the separate instructions to this form. Form **709** (Rev. 1-87)

For a complete 709 form contact the Internal Revenue Service

Sample Irrevocable Trust

THIS AGREEMENT, made this _____ day of _____ 19____ , by and among _____ and _____ residing at _____ (hereinafter referred to as "Grantors") and _____ , a banking institution authorized to do business in the State of _____ (hereinafter referred to as "Trustee").

The Grantors, in consideration of the covenants herein contained, hereby transfer and assign the assets listed on Schedule A annexed hereto to the Trustee, and the Trustee hereby acknowledges receipt of said assets and agrees, for itself and its successors, to hold, administer and dispose of said assets, together with all additions thereto, in trust, upon the following terms and conditions:

WITNESSETH:

FIRST: Irrevocability of Trust

This Trust Agreement is irrevocable. The Grantors hereby relinquished all power to alter, amend or revoke this Trust Agreement in whole or in part. The significance of the irrevocability of this Trust Agreement has been fully explained to the Grantors by their legal counsel. The Grantors intend to sever permanently any control over the assets listed in Schedule A and understand that from and after the creation of the within Trust they shall have no control over the administration or disposition of the assets contained in the Trust.

SECOND: Trust Property—The trust property shall include (a) all of the assets transferred by Grantors to the Trustee; (b) such additional property as may be added to the Trust from time to time. All of said property herein called "the trust fund."

(A) Rights of Trustee—Insurance—The Trustee may but is not required to purchase insurance on the lives of the Grantors which may be acquired as separate policies (covering the life of each Grantor) or as a joint policy (covering the lives of the Grantors jointly). If insurance is purchased by the Trustee the Trustee shall be vested with all right, title, claim benefit and interest in and to such coverages, and is authorized and empowered to exercise and enjoy, for the purposes of this Trust as absolute owner of such insurance coverages, all the options, benefits, rights and privileges pertaining to such insurance coverages including but not limited to:

(1) To exercise all options, rights or elections, including optional modes of settlement, provided for such insurance coverages.

(2) To assign all or part of such insurance coverages in connection with the administration of this Trust, or in the exercise of the powers granted to the Trustee hereunder or vested in the Trustee by operation of law.

(3) To designate and/or change from time to time the beneficiary with respect to such insurance coverages.

(4) To receive any benefits provided for such insurance coverages.

(5) To demand, collect and receive all distributions, shares of surplus, dividends, deposits or additions apportioned to any insurance coverage.

(6) To cancel or to surrender any aforesaid policy for the cash value thereof or for extended term insurance, or to elect to take paid-up insurance with respect to any said policy; to permit any such policy to lapse.

(7) To obtain and secure from the insurance company which had issued any such policy, such advances or loans on account of any such policy as may be available from time to time.

(8) To pledge any such policy as security for the repayment of loans made to this Trust.

(9) The insurance company which has issued any such individual policy is hereby authorized and directed to recognize the Trustee as the absolute owner of and as fully entitled to all options, rights, privileges, and interests with respect to such insurance coverage as may be owned by the Trustee.

(10) With respect to any insurance coverage owned in part by the Trustee on a split-ownership basis, the Trustee, in its sole and absolute discretion, may exercise any and all of those options, benefits, rights and privileges pertaining thereto (including, without limitation, those specifically enumerated above), as shall be applicable to the portion of such insurance coverage owned by the Trustee and the remainder of such options, benefits, rights and privileges shall be exercisable by any other owner(s) thereof.

(11) If required by any insurance company which had issued any policy to discharge said insurance company from any and all liability for any amounts paid to the Trustee, or in accordance with the Trustee's direction, and to agree that no such insurance company shall have any obligation whatsoever to see to the application of any such amounts so paid by it and to agree further that any such insurance company shall be fully protected in taking or permitting any action in reliance on any instrument or document executed by the Trustee in its capacity as Trustee, and that such insurance company shall not incur any liability for so doing.

(B) Payment of Premiums—The Trustee shall be under no obligation to pay the premiums, dues, assessments or other charges which may become due and payable with respect to any insurance coverage which may become owned by this Trust, nor to see that such payments are made, nor to notify the Grantors or any other person that such payments are or will become due, and the Trustee shall be under no liability to anyone in case such premiums, dues, assessments or other charges are not paid, nor for any result of the failure to make such payments; neither the Grantors nor the Trustee shall be deemed, because of the terms of this Trust Agreement, to have entered into any covenant to keep any such insurance coverage in force.

Notwithstanding any provision of this Article to the contrary, the Trustee may pay or apply so much or all of the income and principal of this Trust as the Trustee, in its sole discretion, shall deem advisable, for the premiums, dues, assessments or other charges which may become due and payable with respect to any insurance coverage which may be owned by this Trust any provision of law to the contrary withstanding.

THIRD: Dispositive Provisions—The Trustee shall have and hold the trust fund in TRUST, NEVERTHELESS, to invest and reinvest the same, and to hold and distribute the trust fund as follows:

A. During the Grantors' Lives—During the Grantors' lives:

1. Distribution of Income—For the duration of the Grantors' lives, the Trustee may at any time or from time to time pay or apply so much or all (or none) of the then net income of this Trust (to the extent not expended pursuant to Article Second Paragraphs (A) and (B) or this Article Third Paragraph A.2.) and so much or all (or none) of the principal of this Trust (including all insurance coverages of which the Trustee is the owner) to or for the benefit of any one or more of the Grantors' children living from time to time (whether or not in being at the date of this Trust Agreement), in such amounts or proportions, to the exclusion of any one or more of them, as the Trustee shall determine for any reason whatever and without regard to the interest of any remainderman under this Trust Agreement. At the end of each trust year, the Trustee shall add to the principal of this separate trust any net income not so paid or applied (and not expended as provided in Article Second Paragraphs (A) and (B) or this Article Third Paragraph A.2.) and thereafter the same shall be dealt with as principal of this Trust for all purposes.

2. Annual Rights to Withdraw Principal—Anything in the foregoing to the contrary notwithstanding, during each calendar year prior to both Grantors' deaths, including the year in which this Trust is created and the years in which each Grantor dies, each then-living child of Grantors shall have the absolute right to make withdrawals from the principal of the Trust, in accordance with the following provisions:

(a) Each then-living child of the Grantors may annually withdraw an amount determined by dividing the amount of the contribution by the number of such then-living children; provided, however, that the aggregate amount of such withdrawals by any child of Grantors during any calendar year shall not exceed the lesser of (i) $5,000 per child, or such other amount as may be exempt from treatment as a taxable lapse of a power under IRC §2514(e), as amended from time to time or (ii) the maximum amount allowable as an annual present interest exclusion for gift tax purposes under IRC §2503(b), including such additional exclusion as may be available if the contributing Grantor's spouse consents that any such gift to a child be considered as made one-half by such spouse under IRC §2513, as amended from time to time.

(b) In satisfying the exercise of any right of withdrawal, the Trustee is authorized to make distributions in cash or by an in-kind distribution of other property, including insurance policies.

(c) Withdrawals with respect to a contribution may be made at any time during a two month period commencing on the date of a notice of a contribution considered to be a direct or indirect, actual or deemed transfer made on behalf of a Grantor during that calendar year, including the year in which this Trust is created and the year of a Grantor's death, but in no event shall the amount subject to withdrawal in any calendar year exceed the amounts specified in Subparagraph (a) hereof. If a person entitled to make a withdrawal does not exercise such right in full on or before the expiration of such two month period, the unused portion applicable to that period shall not cumulate to future years, and no payment shall be made in a subsequent year on account of an amount not requested in a prior year.

(d) Withdrawals shall be made by the person entitled to make the same delivering a written request therefor to the Trustee at any time during the above two month period.

(e) In the case of any child of the Grantor's who is a minor, the right of withdrawal granted to such child by this Paragraph shall be exercisable on behalf of such child by his or her guardian or any other person who may act in the child's behalf under state law other than the Grantors.

(f) For purposes of this Paragraph, the term "contribution" or "contribution to the trust fund" shall mean any cash or other assets, including life insurance policies (or any interests therein), which are transferred to the Trustees to be held as part of the trust fund and shall also include any premiums on policies of life insurance (or any interests therein) owned by the Trust which premiums are paid by the Grantors or any other person, directly or indirectly, to the insurance company. The date of the contribution shall be deemed to be the date on which such policy or the property is assigned to the Trust or the date a premium payment is transmitted to the insurance company issuing the policy. The amount of any contribution to the trust fund shall be the value of such contribution for federal gift tax purposes. The initial principal of the trust shall be treated as a "contribution" for purposes of this Paragraph 2.

(g) Immediately upon the creation of this Trust the Trustee shall notify in writing those persons having the right to withdraw principal under this Paragraph (including the guardian or other lawful representative of any minors other than the Grantors) of the existence of the withdrawal right granted and the value of the original contribution, if any, to the Trust, and in addition, the Trustee shall also give written notice to such persons of the date and value of any subsequent contribution to the Trust promptly upon any contribution to the trust fund unless actual notice of the addition already exists. Upon any contribution of property to the Trust, the contributing Grantor shall advise the Trustee in writing the extent to which such property constitutes a contribution, and the Trustee may rely upon such advice without further inquiry and without liability to the Grantors or to any beneficiary hereunder, absent bad faith;

(h) In creating this power it is the intent of the Grantors to create an annual non-cumulative power of invasion which will qualify any transfer of property as a transfer of a present interest under Section 2503(b) of the Internal Revenue Code and will not be treated as a release of such power as that term is defined in Section 2514(e) of said Code.

3. *Collection of Policy Proceeds*—Upon the maturity of any insurance coverage owned by this Trust for any reason, the Trustee shall receive such sum or sums as may be payable thereunder to the Trustee, and shall hold or dispose of the same as provided in Article Fourth. The Trustee is hereby authorized to execute all necessary receipts and releases to the insurance company or companies concerned. Upon being advised of the maturity of any insurance coverage owned by this Trust, the Trustee shall take all necessary steps to collect such sum as may be due the Trustee with respect to such insurance coverage. The Trustee may institute proceedings at law or in equity or otherwise in order to enforce payment to it of any amounts due or to become due under any insurance coverage and the Trustee may do and perform any and all other acts and things which may be necessary for the purpose of collecting any sums which may be or become due and payable to the Trustee under the terms of such insurance coverage provided, however, that the Trustee shall not be required to enter into or maintain any litigation to enforce any such payment unless the Trustee has sufficient funds on hand for that purpose or unless the Trustee has been indemnified to its satisfaction against all expenses and liabilities to which it may, in its judgement, be subjected by any such action on its part.

FOURTH: Upon Grantors' Deaths—Upon the death of both Grantors:

A. So long as any living child of the Grantors' is under twenty-three years of age:

(1) The net income shall be distributed, in quarterly or other installments convenient to the Trustee, to such one or more of the Grantors' descendants in such amount or proportions as the Trustee may from time to time think appropriate; and

(2) As much of the principal as the Trustee may from time to time think desirable may be distributed to such one or more of any of the Grantors' descendants and either shall be paid to that person or shall be applied directly for their benefit.

The Grantors' primary concern is for the care and education of the Grantors' descendants until they become self-supporting and, while the Grantors' general plan is to treat them alike, the Grantors recognize that needs will vary from person to person and from time to time. Accordingly, the Grantors direct that all distributees need not be treated equally or proportionally; that one or more of the eligible distributees may be wholly excluded from any or all periodic distributions; that the pattern followed in one distribution need not be followed in another; and that the Trustee may give such consideration to the other resources of each of the eligible distributees as it may think appropriate.

B. As soon as there is no living child of the Grantors' under twenty-three years of age, the then-remaining principal shall be divided into equal shares, so that there will be one share for each child of the Grantors who is then living and one share for each deceased child of the Grantors' who has descendants then living, with each such deceased child's share being divided equally into further separate shares for such deceased child's living descendants. Each such share of a child or descendant of a deceased child shall be kept invested as a separate trust and thereafter:

(1) During each child's lifetime or during the lifetime of a descendant of a deceased child:

a. The net income from his or her trust shall be paid to him or her, in quarterly or other convenient installments;

b. As much of the principal of his or her Trust as the Trustee may from time to time think desirable—taking into account funds available from other sources may be distributed to him or her and either shall be paid to that person directly or shall be applied for their benefit; and

c. Each child or descendant of a deceased child shall have the right to withdraw up to one-third of the principal of his or her separate trust at any time after reaching twenty-five years of age, up to one-half of the balance thereof at any time after reaching thirty years of age and the entire balance thereof at any time after reaching thirty-five years of age (the maximum amount subject to withdrawal before a child or the descendant of a deceased child reaches thirty-five years of age to be based on the market value of the principal of that child's or descendant of a deceased child's separate trust at the time of his or her first request after reaching each particular age).

(2) At each child's death or at the death of a descendant of a deceased child, any then-remaining principal of his or her separate trust shall be paid:

a. To such one or more persons or organizations—including his or her estate, his or her creditors, and the creditors of his or her estate—on such terms as he or she may appoint by a Will specifically referring to this power of appointment; or, in default of appointment or insofar as it is not effectual,

b. To his or her then-living descendants, per stirpes; or, in default of such descendants,

c. To the Grantors' then-living descendants, per stirpes (any portion thus accruing to a child or descendant of a deceased child for whom principal is then held in trust hereunder to be a deed to and thereafter treated as part of such principal); or, in default of such descendants,

d. To the same persons and in the same proportions as would have inherited such property from the Grantors had the Grantors died interstate, the absolute owners thereof, and residents of the state of (State).

FIFTH: Protective Provision—No interest in income or principal shall be assignable by, or available to anyone having a claim against, a beneficiary before actual payment to the beneficiary.

SIXTH: Situs and Governing Law—The situs of this Trust Agreement shall be in (State) and all questions as to the validity or effect of this deed or the administration of the trusts hereunder shall be governed by the law of (State). The situs of any trust hereunder may be transferred to such other place at any time or times the Trustee considers the transfer in the best interests of the Trust or its beneficiaries thereof. In so doing, the Trustee may resign and appoint a substitute Trustee other than the Grantors, wherever situated, but may remove any substituted Trustee at any time and appoint another other than the Grantors, including itself. Any substitute Trustee may delegate any and all of such substitute Trustee's powers, discretionary or otherwise, to the appointing Trustee.

SEVENTH: Segregation of Property—The Trustee shall not be required to make physical segregation of the property held under this Trust Agreement except when necessary for the purposes of distribution, but may, in its discretion, maintain the separate trusts held under this Trust Agreement as one or more consolidated funds. As to each consolidated fund the division into the various shares or parts comprising such fund need be made only on the Trustee's books of account, in which each separate trust shall be allotted its proportionate part of the principal and income of the fund and charged with its proportionate part of expenses of the fund and charged further with distributions of income and principal of such separate trust.

EIGHTH: Management Provisions—The Trustee is authorized:

(A) To retain and to invest in all forms of real and personal property, including common trust funds operated by the Grantors' Trustee, regardless of (i) any limitations imposed by law on investments by Trustees, (ii) any principle of law concerning delegation of investment responsibility by Trustees or (iii) any principle of law concerning investment diversification;

(B) To compromise claims and to abandon any property which, in the Trustee's opinion, is of little or no value;

(C) To borrow from anyone, even if the lender is the Trustee hereunder, and to pledge property as security for repayment of the funds borrowed;

(D) To sell at public or private sale, to exchange or to lease for any period of time, any real or personal property and to give options for sales or leases;

(E) To make loans to, and to buy property from the Grantors' executors or administrators or the Trustee of any generation-skipping trust of which the Grantors are a deemed transferor;

(F) To join in any merger, reorganization, voting-trust plan or other concerted action of security holders, and to delegate discretionary duties with respect thereto;

(G) To allocate any property received or charges incurred to principal or income or partly to each, without regard to any law defining principal and income;

(H) To distribute in kind and to allocate specific assets among the beneficiaries under any of the trusts under this Agreement of Trust in such proportions as the Trustee may think best, so long as the total market value of any beneficiary's share is not affected by such allocation.

These authorities shall extend to all property at any time held by the Trustee and shall continue in full force until actual distribution of all such property. All powers, authorities, and discretion granted by this deed shall be in addition to those granted by law and shall be exercisable without leave of court.

NINTH: Settlement of Accounts—

(A) The Trustee may from time to time settle its accounts with respect to any separate trust held hereunder by agreement with:

(1) each adult, competent income beneficiary of such separate trust; and

(2) each adult, competent beneficiary who would be entitled to receive some part or all of the principal if such separate trust were to terminate at the time of such agreement;

Such agreement shall bind all persons, whether or not then in being, then or thereafter entitled to any property of the separate trust accounted for, whether principal or income, and shall constitute a complete release and discharge of the Trustee for the acts and proceedings so accounted for.

(B) Nothing contained in this Article shall preclude the Trustee from seeking a judicial settlement of its accounts.

(C) For purposes of this Article, the income beneficiary of a separate trust is each person eligible to receive income distributions, whether or not such beneficiary is in fact receiving distributions of income currently.

251

TENTH: Survivorship—

(A) If any beneficiary of this Trust Agreement dies within thirty (30) days after the death of the second Grantor to die or within thirty (30) days after the death of any person other than the Grantors upon whose death such beneficiary would, but for this Article, be entitled to receive income or principal under this Trust Agreement, then for the purposes of the Trust Agreement, such beneficiary shall be deemed to have predeceased the Grantors or such person other than the Grantors, as the case may be, provided, however, that this Article shall not be construed to permit any suspension of ownership or of the power of alienation, or any other similar rule.

ELEVENTH: Additional Property—

(A) The Grantors or any other person may add property to any separate trust held under this Trust Agreement (i) by lifetime transfers of additional property; (ii) by will; (iii) by naming the Trustee as beneficiary of one or more insurance policies; or (iv) by any other means; provided that such property shall be acceptable to the Trustee. The Trustee may in its absolute discretion decline to accept all or any portion of such additions. Furthermore, if the Trustee agrees to accept any such additions, it shall not be required to retain any property in the form received. Upon receipt and acceptance thereof by the Trustee, any such additions shall be allocated to the separate trust designated by the donor of such additions, or failing such designation, equally to all separate trusts then held under this Trust Agreement.

TWELFTH: Trustees—

(A) No bond or other security shall be required of any Trustee serving hereunder at any time, including any successor, any provision of law to the contrary notwithstanding.

(B) All powers, authority and discretion herein conferred upon the Trustee shall pass to and be exercisable by each successor.

(C) If the Trustee or any successor to it for any reason ceases to act as the Trustee of any trust created hereunder, the income beneficiaries, or during any period that such a beneficiary lacks legal capacity, the guardian (other than a Grantor) of such beneficiary's estate, shall have the right and power to appoint as its successors any bank or trust company that shall have been licensed to engage in trust business for at least five (5) years immediately prior to such appointment and which shall then have capital and surplus of at least Five Million Dollars ($5,000,000.).

(D) Any Trustee may resign by giving thirty (30) days written notice to its successor Trustee named or designated as hereinabove provided, who is qualified and willing to act, and to the income beneficiaries, or where any such beneficiary lacks legal capacity, the guardian (other than a Grantor) of such beneficiary's estate.

Such resignation shall take effect upon the date specified in such notice, whereupon all duties of the Trustee so resigning shall cease, other than the duty to account.

Any Trustee so resigning shall take all steps necessary to effect and perfect the delivery and transfer of all property then held under this Trust Agreement to the successor Trustee. No successor Trustee shall be obliged to examine the accounts, records, and acts of any previous Trustee or any allocations of receipts or disbursements and between principal and income made by any previous Trustee.

THIRTEENTH: Vesting—

Notwithstanding any prior provision of this Trust Agreement to the contrary, the principal of all trusts under this Trust Agreement shall vest absolutely in interest no later than twenty-one years after the death of the survivor of the Grantors, and such of the Grantors' descendants and the spouses of the Grantors' descendants as are living on the date of the execution of this Trust Agreement, and immediately prior to the expiration of twenty-one years after the death of the survivor of the above group any principal which has not vested in interest shall vest absolutely in and become payable to the person then eligible to receive income therefrom.

FOURTEENTH: Death Taxes—

Any death taxes on any future interests shall be paid from principal whenever the Trustee, in the Trustee's sole discretion, thinks best. All federal, state and other death taxes payable because of the Grantors' deaths on any property then held hereunder or on any insurance proceeds or other death benefits payable directly to the Trustee shall be paid out of principal as if they were administration expenses.

FIFTEENTH: Merger With Other Trusts—

In the event that either of the Grantors create another trust or trusts, whether by will or by agreement, the provisions of which are substantially the same as those of the trust or trusts created hereunder, the Trustee in its discretion may, after the Grantors' deaths, merge the trust or trusts created hereunder with such other trust or trusts. In determining whether the provisions of such other trusts are substantially the same as those created hereunder, the discretion of the Trustee shall be conclusive and shall not be subject to judicial review.

SIXTEENTH: Post Mortem Tax Election of Trustee—

Grantors authorize and empower the Trustee to exercise, in its sole and absolute discretion, any elections and options given to it by any provision of the Internal Revenue Code, and other statute or Regulation, state or federal, governing the administration of the Grantors' estates and the Trust hereby created, including but not limited to the following:

(A) **Allocating Generation-Skipping Tax Exemption**—To exercise the power to allocate any exemption from the federal tax on generation-skipping transfers provided by IRC §2631 et. seq. to any property with respect to which a Grantor is treated as the transferor, without regard to whether such property is part of a Grantor's probate estate, and to exclude any such property from such allocation.

(B) **Division of Trusts for Inclusion Ratio Under Generation-Skipping Tax**—To divide any trust created hereunder into separate trusts in order that the inclusion ratio for federal generation-skipping tax purposes for one such trust shall be zero or one.

Grantors' Trustee shall have no liability for or obligation to make compensating adjustments between principal and income or in the interests of the beneficiaries by reason of having made or not made any such election. Any decision made by the Trustee in good faith with respect to the exercise or non-exercise of any such elections shall be binding and conclusive on all interested persons.

IN WITNESS WHEREOF, _____, Grantors have hereunto set their hands and seals and _____, Trustee has hereunto set its hands and seal the day and year above written to execute this instrument.

In the presence of:

_____   _____ (SEAL)
                                            GRANTOR

_____   _____ (SEAL)
                                            GRANTOR

_____   _____
                                            TRUSTEE

                                     by_____

* The Prudential Insurance Company of America and its representatives make no representations as to the tax and legal consequences of this model agreement.

† Counsel should especially consider the effect of community property law on this model agreement.

NOTE: A Life Underwriter should be familiar with the terms of this sample agreement and the manner in which it may be used. However, a Life Underwriter may not draw agreements for clients and should not suggest that the clients draw their own. A duly licensed attorney is the only person who may give legal advice and only an attorney is qualified to draw an agreement designed to solve the problems of a particular situation.

NOTICE TO TRUST BENEFICIARY OF WITHDRAWAL RIGHT

(DATE)

To   <u>(Beneficiary or Beneficiary's Legal Representative)</u>

Address _____

_____

This is to advise you that a gift of $_____ was made on <u>(date)</u>_____ to the (Grantors')_____ Trust dated _____.

Pursuant to Article _____ Paragraph _____ of such Trust, you as a beneficiary may have the right to demand a withdrawal of a portion of the principal from the Trust under the terms and conditions thereof.

To exercise your right of withdrawal, please respond in writing to the undersigned Trustee, at the address below within two months of the date of this notice. Any questions you have about this right of withdrawal or its exercise should be directed to the undersigned Trustee.

Yours truly,

Trustee

By_____

Trustee   _____

Attention   _____

Address   _____

_____

Index